CW00972712

RELUCTANT REBELS

The 1972 Housing Finance Act and its
Political implications in South Shields

Iain Malcolm

Cover photograph by Alan White of Trac Photographics

Cover design: Peter Chapman

Published by Durham City Publishing Company,

9 Hill Top, Esh, Durham.

ISBN: 0953465 52 7

Every act of rebelling expresses a nostalgia for innocence and an appeal to the essence of being... **Albert Camus**

To my Uncle Billy

Acknowledgments

During the May 1978 local Elections, my father introduced me to Ernie Mackley, our local Councillor who was seeking re-election to South Tyneside Council. As a young boy, I readily delivered his leaflets around Simonside and felt the sense of injustice when both Ernie and my father lost their seats in the anti-Labour landslide of that year. Both men, in their own way had served their local communities and both had lost their seats because of the unpopularity of the Callaghan Government that was sweeping across Britain at the time. As I nursed my disappointment, I had no way of knowing that a decade later, at the age of just 21, I would in a small way right the wrong by being elected myself to serve as a member of South Tyneside Council.

Following his defeat, and knowing my interest in local politics, Ernie gave me a momento of the campaign, a copy of a book entitled 'The New Local Authorities, management and structure' — It was hardly gripping stuff but Ernie assured me — "It will come in handy one day".

Flicking through the book, I came across a press cutting tucked inside, with the headline, 'Rents decision splits Labour'. Apparently, the Labour Group on the former South Shields town Council had decided by one vote not to stand in the way of Officials preparing for the introduction of 'fair rents'.

So began my interest in the Housing Finance Act of 1972. I was helped by the fact that my father, like myself, rarely threw away papers and so I was able to begin to piece together the events surrounding the implementation of the Rent Act in South Shields in 1972.

This book has been a long time in the making. I originally wrote a manuscript on the subject for my BA (Hons) Degree in 1989. At that time I interviewed a number of people who were prominent during the Rent Act episode including — Jim Florence, Billy Malcolm, Liz Diamond, Ivor Richardson and Jim Doneghan, all of whom have sadly since died. I also interviewed Jack Grassby, Jim Davison, Ken Reid,

Bob Growcott, Mike Peel and Sep Robinson, all of whom gave their time freely and answered my endless questions with patience and good grace. Malcolm Campbell was at that time unavailable for interview. Sadly Ernie Mackley died in 1988 so I was never able to record his own private thoughts.

Ten years later, a number of people encouraged me to consider turning the manuscript into a book. In order to expand upon the original manuscript I received written comments from George Smith, Stan Smith and Jim Riddle. I also had an opportunity to interview Malcolm Campbell, Richard (Dickie) Barry and Neil Bonnar. Again, I am grateful for the patience shown in answering my questions on this occasion.

In addition, I wish to place on record my thanks to the Tyne and Wear Archives Service and also the staff of the Libraries of Gateshead, MBC, Newcastle City Council, Sunderland City Council and Tower Hamlets Council for their support during my initial research. I am, as always, in debt to the staff of South Tyneside Local History Library, in particular Keith Bardwell and Doris Johnson for their encouragement and assistance.

I am grateful to the South Shields Labour Party and the South Shields Trades Union Council for allowing me access to their Minute Books for my research. The Labour Party Minute Books are now stored in the Central Library, South Shields.

Finally, I wish to thank Michael Lloyd and Nick Davvy for reading the proofs and providing helpful comments and advice, and also my long suffering family who have had to endure endless talk and discussion about the events of 1972!

Ernie was right, that book did come in useful.

Introduction

Clay Cross is something rather special. It really is. I think everyone in Britain, in the Labour Movement and outside, is full of sympathy and admiration for the stand that David Skinner and his colleagues have taken.

Ted Short, Labour's Deputy Leader, Party Conference 1973

Like the author of this book, I was fed and watered on local politics by my father who was an NUM activist. My family helped build up the Clay Cross Labour Party and my elder brother Dennis was the first Leader of the Labour Council. Like the author it was therefore not surprising that I would become, at 21, the youngest member of my local Council.

Clay Cross Council in 1970 had that rare distinction in that we did not have a single opposition member in the Council Chamber. We presented a radical manifesto to help pensioners, schoolchildren and the Council tenants of our District and, to a considerable extent, we succeeded in our aim. We involved ourselves in our local communities and were rewarded with a turnout of over 62% at the local elections.

We were not just determined, we were also ingenious. When the statutory incomes policy prohibited an increase in wages for the council's manual workers, we promoted them all to foremen. We frustrated Thatcher's best-laid plans to deprive young people of free school milk — at first we used the product of the penny rate and when this proved insufficient, we used the Chairman's entertainment allowance, suitably increased.

Every now and then, socialists, like those referred to in this book, will defy the stale local government routine of tea and biscuits and conferences to implement their election promises and proudly proclaim Municipal Socialism in their District.

When the Heath Government published its White Paper, 'A Fair Deal for Housing', it was clear that the Clay Cross Labour Party and the Tory

Government had different ideas as to the word 'fair'. The Tories' intention was to make 'financially better-off' tenants contribute towards housing rebates for the 'less well-off'. This of course was accompanied by a reduction in the Exchequer subsidies to the local authority. Clay Cross Council had prided itself on implementing a low-rent policy and it was therefore obvious that we would not countenance raising the rents.

Across the whole country, Labour Councils made clear that they would not implement the Rent Act — unfortunately local circumstances saw those same councils back-track on their earlier pledges.

But Clay Cross — backed by the residents — remained steadfast. Our refusal to implement the Rent Act led to the District Auditor imposing surcharges upon the eleven Labour Councillors and threatening action over alleged council 'mismanagement' in 1973. We were also removed from office.

This book chronicles the 'struggles' in the South Shields Labour Party but it also gives a snapshot of how the local Trades Council was able to influence the events as they unfolded.

Like the South Shields Labour Party, we in Clay Cross had been elected on a clear mandate to oppose the Housing Finance Act. The introduction of national policies being forced on locally elected members is bad enough, but when the politics is Tory legislative dogma, it's like a fishbone in the back of the throat. I am proud of my former colleagues on Clay Cross Council and do not regret the principled stand we took at the time. In politics you have to stand up for your beliefs, hang the consequences.

I recommend this a must for the people of South Shields. Like the people of Clay Cross, you should be proud of your history — in a small way you played a part in destroying the worst piece of Tory legislation ever put up.

Enjoy.

David Skinner
Clay Cross Councillor, 1970-74

Preface

A leaflet published by the South Shields Federation of Tenants Associations in 1972 talks of how Council house tenants in the town could fight back against the Heath Government's 'Fair Rents Bill'. By taking direct action and going on a rent strike, the Federation claimed that the tenants would be able to defeat the Government and force a retreat on the rent issue.

The leaflet ended with these stirring words:

> *Fight back, refuse to pay the rent increase and you can change the law.... The miners did.... the dockers did.... and so can you!*

The election defeat of Harold Wilson's Labour administration in 1970 left a lot of activists disillusioned, although some would argue that this defeat was inevitable. Wilson's Government was characterised by such events as strict immigration control legislation, a wage freeze, cuts in health spending, support for the United States' bombing of Vietnam, as well as legislation designed to curb union powers. These events (in varying degrees) resulted in a mass exodus of members from the Labour Party. As a consequence, parties such as the International Socialists (now the Socialist Workers Party), -the Socialist Labour League (later the Workers Revolutionary Party), and the Communist Party grew in strength as did single-issue groups such as the Campaign for Nuclear Disarmament, the Child Poverty Action Group and Shelter.

This period of British political history was also a time of immense left-wing agitation influenced by such people as Tariq Ali and Daniel Cohn-Bendit (student revolutionaries), Jerry Rubin (the father of American Hippies) and Herbert Marcuse (widely regarded as the father of the new left).

We could argue that such events as the 1968 student demonstrations in France, the draft issue in the United States, the Hippy Movement, the emergence of women's and gay rights issues and the spread of claimants unions in the 1969-70 period were associated with this new left philosophy.

South Shields was in no way insulated against these influences and in the early 1970s, it accommodated active cells or branches of the Socialist Labour League (SLL), International Marxist Group (IMG) and International Socialist (IS) members. Whilst the Communist Party had a small presence, its members tended to be older and it was in danger of withering away locally.

The rebellious decision in 1972 of the South Shields Labour Party to refuse to implement the Housing Finance Bill if it became law needs to be seen in the context of the above framework. It was spurred on by the success of the miners in their 1972 dispute, the very popular Upper Clyde Shipbuilders occupation (which brought Jimmy Reid to national prominence), the Ford Strike of 1970-71, as well as the growing confidence of trade union militants in general.

This book will examine the Act and its introduction in the Town in three main ways. Examining the Act itself — what it sought to achieve and why it was so controversial; placing the Act into a local perspective by examining the political history of South Shields; and finally by detailing the events as they happened. From the local Labour Party being out of control to the decision of eleven Labour Councillors to break ranks and side with the official opposition in the Council Chamber and vote to implement the Act.

I am not intending to provide a complete study; merely an introduction to an interesting period of local political history, which, I feel, needs to be recorded. The material was gathered from private collections of newspapers and reports and from interviews and discussions with people who were prominent at the time. It does not seek to place judgement on the actions of any individuals — I merely wish to record them. As such I hope that the book will provide an informative and valuable introduction to a fascinating period of local politics.

Contents

Chapter 1

A Fair Deal for Housing

These proposals will give the greatest help to areas of greatest need.
Subsidies will be concentrated on those areas where they will
stimulate the clearance of slums.

Government White Paper: 'A Fair Deal for Housing'

Before the General Election of June 1970, the Conservative Party published a pamphlet outlining its central objectives in housing if it was returned to power. Although the Tories claimed at the time that their main aim was the establishment of a 'fair rent', opponents were quick to point out that the real intention was to cut subsidies to housing. It took the new Heath Government just over a year to publish the White Paper, 'A Fair Deal for Housing'. The White Paper was only one of a number going through the Commons in 1972, but for the 17,000 Council house tenants in South Shields it was by far the most sensitive. If the Bill became Law, they, along with their families and most people living in private rented unfurnished accommodation, would face a radically different housing scene.

The Bill proposed to raise enough money from Council tenants to pay for slum clearance and rent rebates to poorer council tenants and to give help to over a million tenants in unfurnished private accommodation — whose rents would be decontrolled but who would receive direct help from the Government for the first time. In 1972, the Government would be spending £350m subsiding Council housing. Most of the subsidy went to five million council-owned properties and only a fraction went to slum clearance. The Bill sought to reverse this by placing an emphasis on Council rents as the principle funding mechanism.

However, the Bill also attempted to encourage people to buy their Council houses. One Minister at the time said:

A person who can afford an economic rent or a fair rent for his Council house will prefer to buy. Some Council house rents could easily reach the same figure as mortgage repayments. [1]

Indeed the Bill itself said:

Home ownership is the most rewarding form of house tenure. It satisfies a deep and natural desire on the part of the Householder to have independent control of the home that shelters him and his family. It gives him the greatest possible security against the loss of his home; and particularly against price changes that may threaten his ability to keep it. If the householder buys his house on mortgage, he builds up a steady saving capital asset for himself and his dependents. In this country, the existence of a strong building society movement helps him realise these advantages. [2]

The implications of the changes would be that Council tenants would face an increase in their rents higher than the town had ever previously experienced, to be followed a year later by a further increase since the Government considered most Council rents were below the 'fair' level.

To soften the blow, a universal rent rebate scheme would be implemented and both Council and tenants in private rented accommodation would be able to claim if their income was judged to be too low for the rents they would in future be paying. In South Shields many people living in medium-rented properties and earning relatively 'normal wages' would find their rents leaping up in the two years following 1972.

The Government was therefore aiming to ensure a 'fair rent' which ultimately meant one unsubsidised by the Government.

In Appendix 2 of the White Paper the mechanism that was to be adopted by Local Authorities in calculating the rent increases was outlined. The Bill instructed local Authorities to collect an extra £26 rent per Council house in the 12 months from April 1972. The Government gave Local Authorities some discretion as to how to achieve this. Some Councils decided to raise their rents from the 1 April 1972 (before rebates were introduced and before the Bill had actually received Royal Assent), so that their tenants would pay on average 50p a week extra for one year.

2

In South Shields, the Progressive-controlled Council (a local independent Rent and Ratepayer's Association) had a majority in the Chamber of only two, and with an eye on the May elections postponed raising the rents. George Smith, the Housing Chairman argued that the Council would not increase the rents because the Bill may still have been altered and he considered it wrong to ask people to pay the rent increase before the rebate scheme came into effect. [3]

If Councils delayed increasing the rents, then the shortfall obviously had to be met by larger rent increases later in the year.

Page 32 (Clause iii) of the White Paper, advised that the Town Council initially determine what constituted a 'fair rent'. However, this decision had to be checked by the local Rent Scrutiny Committee whose members were derived from the Rent Assessment Panel — the latter of whom were appointed by the Government. Previously the Panel had only dealt with problems of rent levels in the private sector. Under the Bill there was no appeal against the Panel's decision.

In South Shields, the Council ran its own rent rebate scheme for those tenants whose rents were particularly high (generally those houses less than four years old). Under the terms of the Bill, the rebate scheme would be far more generous. Its mechanics were simple — a family man living in a two-bedroomed post-war Council House would at the time be paying a rent of roughly £2.75 (including 91p rates). Following implementation of the Bill, his rent would increase to £3.80 (of which 91p would be rates) — leaving a 'net rent' of just under £3. If he earned £30 a week, he would receive no rebate, if he earned £25 he could claim 69.5p rebate a week. At £20 the rebate was £1.54$\frac{1}{2}$p, at £12 a week the man would pay no rent but would still have his 91p rates to cover.

But Local Authorities were mainly concerned that under the Bill more people would be eligible for rebates (it was calculated some 40 per cent more) and the Councils themselves were required to pay their share. In the first year of implementation, the Government would pay 90 per cent of all rebates claimed, but after four years this would drop to 75 per cent, with the remainder being met by the rates. [4]

*Signing the completion papers for the first council house sale since 1956.
(left to right) Ald. W. Newby; Cllr. G. Smith; R.S. Young, Town Clerk;
Cllr. J. L. Capstick; John Drewry, Director of Housing.
Photo: Shields Gazette*

Local Councils would therefore be required to finance a large proportion of the new rebates. In more prosperous areas this would not have been a problem, but in South Shields, a relatively deprived area, the financial burden on the Council would be greater.

The Labour Party objected to the Bill, considering it an extension of the Means Test, and they feared that rent increases would mean some people paying two and half times the gross value of their homes.

The Progressives generally supported the Bill since one of its objectives, they argued, was the 'transfer of subsidy from bricks and mortar to people'.[5]

George Smith became Chair of the Housing Committee when the Progressives took control of the Authority in 1969. He is credited with being one of the architects of the 'Right to buy' policy for Council tenants. Today he recalls:

> *At this time a lot of people were living in council houses who were relatively well off and were being subsidised by people in the private sector, some of whom were in poor circumstances, so the Housing Bill was a rather crude attempt to rectify the balance and give subsidy to where it was needed.*

> *The Progressives wished to encourage the purchase of the council houses by the tenants which would save the subsidy, reduce the loan debt and repair costs and the tenant would then have a 'stake' in the community. By the end of 1972 we had made a start and had sold over 200 houses and there were over 1,000 in the pipeline.*

Smith still maintains that the policy was right:

> *Looking at the estates now and seeing the improvements that have been made there is no doubt that this was the right policy for the town.* [6]

But Arthur Blenkinsop, MP for South Shields speaking in a Commons debate on the Housing Finance Bill, warned that old music-hall jokes about Council housing would return.

> *Some of us were proud of the fact that in the 1949 legislation, we cut out the expression 'working class' and insisted that a local housing authority had general housing responsibility.*

> *The objective now, clearly, is to force authorities back into the narrow confines of insisting that they should provide only for the lowest income groups, so that it is made clear to everyone in a neighbourhood that those are the people who live in Council estates. The old music hall jokes about Council houses would return.*

Blenkinsop was particularly critical of the rebate scheme for those who would be unable to pay the increased rent. He claimed that only a small number of people in areas like South Shields, who were entitled to rebates were likely to apply for them.

I fear that we shall return to segregated groups in our town, with some slum clearance estates such as we had before the war — something which many of us thought we had at last managed to leave behind.[7]

The Bill also came in for criticism from the Child Poverty Action Group. The CPAG argued that many relatively poor tenants, living in private accommodation and paying an inflated rent, would be too frightened of harassment to recoup the excess by temporarily not paying rent — as the Law would allow. They warned that the Housing Bill would provide greater opportunities for exploitation in the private sector.[8]

South Shields lies between the urban centres of Wearside and North Tyneside. By-passed by major roads and the Tyne Tunnel, it is today the centre of civic affairs for South Tyneside Council. Anciently know as 'Le Sheels', its history is dominated by the sea, salt and later the local colliery. Although it is politically a working-class town, which experienced in the past some appalling housing and working conditions, it does have some beautiful scenery and a magnificent coastline which is now under the guardianship of the National Trust.

In 1834 the local Burghers unsuccessfully petitioned to Parliament for the town to have County Borough status. However, in 1850 the Charter of Incorporation was granted and in November of that year three wards were created (Jarrow, Westoe and South Shields) which in turn elected a total of 15 Councillors. These Councillors together with eight un-elected Alderman were the first South Shields Town Council. Civic life was very much a gentlemanly and business-orientated affair. None of the Councillors or Alderman officially 'represented' any political party, although early editions of the Shields Gazette recall that there was a thriving 'Liberal cause' in the town at this time. Indeed, following the Great Reform Act in 1832, South Shields commenced electing its own Member of Parliament and in the Election of that year a Liberal, Robert Ingham, had the distinction of being the town's first MP, although we should remember that the franchise was limited, Ingham having been elected with only 205 votes.[9]

Such has been the radical tradition of the town that South Shields has never in its political history elected a Conservative to represent it at Westminster. This radicalism saw the Liberal Party dominate the parliamentary scene until the 1929 General election when the Labour Party was finally able to capture the seat with their schoolmaster candidate, James Chuter Ede.

Locally, working-class feeling was initially expressed through the Trades Council, one of the oldest in the country having been formed in 1872, and it was originally through the Liberal Party that the Trades Council operated. However, in 1892, the Trades Council supported one of their officers, John Lisle, who was a tailor in the town, to stand for election in the Laygate Ward. Lisle was successful and was joined a year later by Joseph Abbott, a small shop-owner and a supporter of the Independent Labour Party. The Shields Gazette, however, neglected to mention his 'socialist credentials' and even in announcing the result did not mention the support he had received from the Trades Council.[10]

With the formation of the Labour Representation Committee (LRC) in 1900, South Shields politics was destined to change. In 1906 the local Trades Council and LRC formed the Municipal Representation Committee. They began campaigning for Council seats almost immediately, although it was not until after the First World War that a truly united front was presented, with official Labour Candidates seeking election in every Local Council ward. Finally, the Shields Gazette was moved to accept the emergence of local party politics by announcing the political party that the candidate stood for. However, those opposed to the Labour Party still refused to officially describe themselves as anything other than 'Shopkeeper', 'Doctor', 'Businessman' or 'Gentleman'.

Following the 1919 Municipal Elections in which the Labour Party gained three seats (including West Park), the local Liberal Association became concerned.

After the 1919 municipal elections, the local Liberals began to urge in their party a more combative approach to the Labour Party and its avowed intention to 'bring politics into local Government', as Alderman

Kaye put it: 'I do not believe in a Town Council being a political organisation but at the same time the other side do' [11]

But it was not until the 1925 local elections that Labour's opponents faced reality and presented a right-wing united front alternative under the name 'Moderates', whose principal claim was to serve the people of South Shields without allegiance to any political party.

Following the 1931 local elections, the Labour Party had a majority in the Council Chamber for the first time in their history. Much of the credit for the achievement must go to Aaron Ernest Gompertz who helped create, through his administrative skill, a powerful Labour Group on the Council. Gompertz was very much the dominant figure locally, Agent for Chuter Ede in every General Election between 1929 and 1959; he was also Secretary of the Labour and Trades Council — a full-time position.

Gompertz was of Dutch-Jewish parentage. He first won a seat on the Council in 1932 and became an un-elected Alderman in 1946. When Labour was in danger of losing a seat in the local elections later that same year, Gompertz resigned his seat on the Aldermanic bench and promised the electors of Horsley Hill that if elected he would never again serve as an Alderman. Gompertz duly won the seat and stood by his promise. Eventually becoming Mayor of South Shields in 1953 — 'the first Jewish Mayor' he is reported to have remarked. He was a teetotaller, non-smoker and vegetarian and for over 40 years he dedicated his life to the cause of the Labour Party.

Controlling the joint Labour and Trades Council machine as well as access to the local MP, Gompertz had immense influence and power in the Labour Party (Labour Leader Clem Attlee attended the Mayor's Sunday Parade in 1953).

By 1960, Ede (who had been the town's MP since 1929), announced that he would be retiring. Gompertz, by now in his seventies, faced unprecedented opposition to his management style from young stalwarts, most notably Ernie Mackley (who had an eye on the Parliamentary seat).

Billy Malcolm — a young Councillor in awe of Gompertz — admitted

8

Cllr. A. Ernest Gompertz   *Photo: South Tyneside Libraries*

that his style could at times be authoritarian and uncompromising.

On the 1 March 1960 at the Annual Meeting of the Labour and Trades Council, Mackley's supporters tabled a motion that would, in effect, destroy Gompertz's power-base within the Party machine. Ivor Richardson, a long-standing member of the Labour Party, recalls telling his wife that he was off that evening to witness a 'political assassination'. It was, recalled Richardson '…a sad and bitter meeting'.[12]

Mackley's motion was passed by a large majority of 47-18. Gompertz, with quiet but determined dignity, resigned the following day from the Town Council and relinquished all his public offices.

It was a sad end to a man who gave his life to the cause of the Labour Party in the town, but he displayed no bitterness to his former 'comrades'. He died in 1968 but elderly people in the town still remember with affection 'Gompy', and in his memory the Secretary's Office in the Labour Party rooms is named in his honour.

The election of the Labour Government with a working majority in 1945 saw the local party lose control of the Town Council despite facing a divided opposition — the Moderates and the Rent and Ratepayers' Association (RARAMA). [13] A year later the Moderates changed their name to Progressives in an attempt to be more electorally popular but the Labour Party regained control of the Council. Realising that a divided opposition helped only Labour, the Progressives and RARAMA merged for the 1947 elections but the Labour Party held on to control of the local Council until 1950 when RARAMA had the majority of seats in the Council Chamber. Their term of office was short-lived. Labour regained control in 1952.

It was not until 1969, when the opposition had changed their name (once again to Progressive), that Labour's long rule in the Town Hall came to a shattering end.

Politically, whichever party controls Whitehall will ultimately lose the Town Halls. South Shields proved to be no exception to this rule. In 1964 when Harold Wilson entered Number 10 as the first Labour Prime Minister for thirteen years, Labour locally enjoyed a brief honeymoon with the electorate.

By 1965, Labour lost two Council seats and in 1967 a further two. In 1968 three electoral defeats gave the Progressive Association hope of a breakthrough. It duly came in 1969. Despite Labour's leaflets proclaiming that they had built 11,433 Council houses since 1945, built

23 new schools and provided concessionary fares on local transport, the Government's unpopularity had sealed the local Labour Party's fate.[14]

Prominent Labour members who lost their seats included Albert Elliott in Simonside, Mrs. Jane Fry in Brinkburn, Harry Malcolm in Tyne Dock and Jim Florence in Rekendyke. Returning to Council politics was George Smith who later became the Chair of Housing (his brother Stan assumed the Council Leadership).[15]

Progressive domination of the town's affairs was characterised by the sale of Council housing (bitterly opposed by the Labour Party) and selling of land for private development — still a sore point with local Labour figures today.

The former Leader of the Authority, Stan Smith, says today:

We could not win a majority on the Council unless a large number of council tenants voted for us. The problem was that there were too many council houses. It seems that all the building land belonged to the Council and the Church Commissioners. The only way out of the difficulty was to sell the Council houses and land. This is what we did.[16]

Cllr. Stan Smith   Photo: Shields Gazette

By the 1971 local elections, the Progressives were able to claim that there had been no rent increase for two years, a Grammar School for Girls was nearing completion and 600 pre-war homes had been modernised. However, the election of Edward Heath as Conservative Prime Minister in 1970 had turned the tables locally. In May 1971 it was Labour's 'Night of Glory' as six Progressive seats fell. Among the new Labour intake were Bob Growcott, Secretary of the South Shields Labour Party and Labour Party Women's Section Activist Lilian Jordison.

Also elected for the first time was Malcolm Campbell in the Rekendyke Ward. Campbell had distinguished himself as a strong trade unionist and as a result on more than one occasion had been victimised and blacklisted. An active member of the GMWU, in the 1960s he established a taxi 'Co-operative' business in South Shields, bringing together more than 40 drivers, with Malcolm having the hackney name 'Red 1' — '…but the lads were all in the Union', recalls Campbell.

One of Campbell's first acts as a Councillor saw him leading an occupation by parents of the Council education offices against the conditions their children were being taught in as a result of building work being undertaken at Laygate School. 'I think from that day, Jim Doneghan (the Labour Party Education Spokesman) hated my guts because he felt I had acted inappropriately.'[17]

The 1971 elections reduced the Progressive majority in the Council Chambers to only two seats.

The Housing Finance Bill, which was nearing completion in Parliament, was proving to be a controversial issue in local political circles. Although the Progressives were in favour of the Bill's recommendations, they refused to raise the rents on the 1 April 1972 by 50p, thus ensuring that whichever party took control after the May elections would be faced with increasing the rents by £1 in October.

It is surprising how little appears to have been done to activate local tenants earlier, especially in light of developments when the Labour Council threatened not to implement the Act.

Although the Conservative Government had made known its intentions almost immediately upon election in 1970, it was not until December 1971 that the local Trades Council began to discuss how they should formulate a campaign to oppose the Bill. In addition, it was not until the

12

31st December 1971 that the local Labour Party distributed over 18,000 leaflets warning tenants of the Bill's recommendations.[18]

Such inactivity however needs to be seen in relation to other issues dominant at the time. Britain was gripped in the debate on whether to enter the Common Market, and the Miners Union had voted for a national strike against the governments pay award. That seems to have taken the impetus away from the rent issue as far as the Trades Council was concerned. The Labour Party was far more concerned with the Local Government Bill, which was also making its way through Westminster. This recommended the abolition of South Shields County Borough Council and proposed its amalgamation with Boldon UDC, Hebburn UDC and Jarrow UDC Councils into a new Metropolitan Borough.

If the Labour movement appeared to ignore the rent issue, the Progressive Association did not. They knew that whilst they supported the principles contained in the Bill, they had to plan very carefully its implementation. With a majority of only two on the Council they could not raise the rents **and** hope to retain power at the May 1972 Council elections.

George Smith, the then Progressive Chair of the Housing Committee, recalls:

'There was no chance that the Progressives would agree to increase the rents on the 1 April by 50p with the election in May, before the passing of the Bill and before the implementation of the much more generous rent rebate scheme.'[19]

Sidney Curry, the Council Treasurer, who had a reputation as a very cautious man, outlined the situation to the Housing Committee on 12 January 1972. A net annual increase

Cllr. George Smith
Photo: Shields Gazette

13

of £26 per household was required under the Bill, if they raised the rents on April 1 then only an increase of 50p per week was needed. Failure to raise the rents on this date, for whatever reason, would mean a higher increase in October in order to make up the shortfall. The position for the Progressives was clear — either they raised the rents and eased the burden and perhaps lost power in May, or they delayed setting the rent increase until October and thus had a greater chance of retaining control of the Authority.[20]

George Smith recalls that he advised his Labour counterpart, Billy Malcolm, that the Progressives would not increase the rents until the rebate scheme was in place.

Billy Malcolm argued that the decision by the Progressive Party not to raise the rents was a clear political act intended to ensure that their candidates did not go into the local elections with a rent increase on their hands.[21] However, today, George Smith still maintains that it would have been unfair to have raised the rents before the Rent Bill had actually become law.

The 12 January 1972 Housing Committee was interesting because it was the first time in the Council Chamber that the Labour Party stated publicly that they were not in favour of implementing the Bill if it became law, although their Housing spokesman, Billy Malcolm spoke in a personal capacity when he said that he was in favour of **all** Local Authorities taking a united stand and refusing to implement the Bill.[22]

The March meeting of the full Council saw the Bill debated one again. The Council's Housing Revenue Account recorded a surplus of £200,000 and a Labour Party motion attempted to stop the Progressives transferring this into the Council's General Rate Fund. Instead they wanted the money given back to the tenants through 'free rent weeks'. The Progressives maintained that to give 'free rent weeks' would be cruel because tenants would have had to pay back the money under the terms of the Fair Rents Bill.

Billy Malcolm moving the Labour motion described the fair rents proposals as a 'naked class Bill':

It reveals its nakedness with a verbiage of legal talk which confuses even the experts. But we do know that in the end both the ratepayer and the Council house tenant will have to bear a far greater burden for Council housing than they ever did before.

He argued that it was unfair not to grant free-rent weeks because the Bill was not law and may not even become law since following the May elections a majority of Councils in the country might be Labour-controlled and might refuse to implement the Act.

But George Smith said that Council tenants were being used as a political pawn. The surplus was due to the Government's cutting interest rates:

If we agree to give them three rent-free weeks then we would have to recoup the money over the next 15 months.

Smith argued that he had consulted with the Government's Regional Office who maintained that the granting of free-rent weeks would constitute a reduction of rent and would have to be added back to the rent in the next financial year.

Labour's motion was defeated by 30 votes to 29.[23]

The 4 April monthly meeting of the local Labour Party's Management Committee discussed the issue of non-implementation. It had been left to the April meeting, the minutes recall, because of a mix-up in dates for when notices of motion could be submitted for consideration. Accordingly, the Chairman Murtagh Diamond and Secretary Bob Growcott had tabled a motion supporting non-implementation as an option 'if or when the Bill becomes law'. The minutes do not record any dissent. The South Shields Labour Party was one of the first Labour Party Constituencies in the North East to announce its refusal to implement the Bill if it became law.[24]

The Local Labour Party also agreed a motion to 'honour' any applications from tenants who had registered a desire to purchase their Council houses up until 4 May (the day of the Council elections).

The Labour Leader Ald. Mackley announced in the Shields Gazette, the following evening that if the Labour Party were returned to power at the May Council elections, they would not implement the Bill; a Tory Commissioner, he maintained, would have to be brought into the town to do the job.[25]

This sent a shock wave through the town. Never had Labour's opposition to the Bill been described in such detail and with the added authority of the Group Leader. The electorate were given a clear lead as to Labour's position. The Progressive Association however was unimpressed. The following day they called upon Mackley to resign as a magistrate, claiming that he advocated breaking the law and thus was not a fit person to be Deputy Chairman of the Towns Magistrates bench.[26]

On 26 April, the Full Council debated yet again the Rent Bill issue. This time, 17 Labour Councillors had signed a notice of motion deploring the Fair Rents Bill and demanding that the Council make appropriate representation to the Government Minister. They again voiced concerns that the Authority would become a mere 'rent agency' under the Bill with no planning role. In what the Shields Gazette described as a 'heated debate', John McKee, the Finance Committee Chairman, said that 'propaganda' peddled by the Labour Party had made people believe that rents would double under the Act. Subsidies, he said, would in future go to those in the greatest need rather than to everyone. But Biddick Hall Councillor Jim Davidson, who later resigned over the issue, said that the Bill would lead to the 're-emergence of the ghettos and slums'.[27]

The Council carried a Progressive amendment welcoming the Fair Rents Bill.

The Late 1960s and early 1970s is an interesting period in the history of the South Shields Constituency Labour Party. Not only was it a period of Progressive control of the Town Council with the implementation of policies which even today cause consternation amongst Labour stalwarts, but it also saw the formal separation between the Labour Party and the Trades Union Council.

During the post-1945 period, South Shields had one of the few joint TUC/Labour Party arrangements in the country — with a complex constitution to back it up. The 1966 Labour Government had offended many trade unionists and resulted in the emergence of many fringe and extremist groups, and it also led to a number of trade unionists being openly hostile to the Labour Party.

Accordingly at the beginning of 1970, many activists felt that it was a good time at which to formally separate. Local trades unionists would also have been encouraged to move for separation since this course of action was recommended by the TUC.

Jim Florence, a long-serving Labour Party Stalwart, who may well have become the Council Leader had it not been for his election defeat at the polls in 1968 — was the main instigator of the split between the two organisations. Florence said that he was motivated primarily because he believed that the trades union movement was not receiving its fair share of attention at the joint meetings. 'Industrial business was always dealt with first', he recalls, '...it was always just a few items of correspondence and then the rest of the meeting would be taken up with "political business", which was always considered the more important'.[28]

Mike Peel, at the time a member of the NUM and now a senior Welfare Rights Officer for South Tyneside Council, recalls being disgusted at the extent to which arguments in the joint meetings were spitefully personalised and bad-tempered and drew on malicious instincts. 'Neither faction could claim a monopoly of virtue', said Peel. Indeed Peel maintains that the personalisation of legitimate political disagreement and the attempts to vilify opponents led to a legacy of bad feeling in both camps and was a crucial factor in what occurred in relation to the Rent Act issue.[29]

There was also the additional problem of how to deal with those trade unionists who were not Labour Party members. The Labour establishment was always very uneasy with people attending the joint meetings who were 'political opponents'. People like Jim and Dorothy Riddle, members of the National Union of Tailor and Garment Workers but also active Communists; Hugh Nicol, a member of the AUEW Trade Union, but also on the Central Committee of the Socialist Labour League, and Jim Rowson, a member of the Lecturers Union, but not a member of any political party.

Jim Riddle recalls even being barred from entering the joint meetings because he was a Communist.

Peel also argues that we cannot underestimate the pressures which were probably brought to bear by such organisations as the Communist Party, which actively sought a separation of the two organizations as a direct consequence of such political manoeuverings by the Labour 'elite'.

Jim Florence maintains that they perhaps simply could not ignore the fact that there was a growing division between the two: on the one hand there were local politicians who resented younger Councillors like himself who had strong party loyalties and a belief in the socialist cause, and on the other trade unionists who were increasingly becoming suspicious of the Labour Party.

The Town Hall in the early 1970s, he recalls, was very much an exclusive club:

'Older Councillors were always very unhappy with resolutions adopted by the local Party, they never considered such resolutions as official Party policy. The Local Council Leadership wrote the election manifesto and acted in the way that they thought best. But in the face of growing rebelliousness from the younger members, such ideas could not be contained'.[30]

The vote to formally separate received the necessary two-thirds majority at the Joint Annual Meeting on 17 February 1970 and the two organisations split. Jack Grassby became the first Secretary of the independent Trades Union Council with Jim Florence acting as the Chairman.

However, there can be little doubt that this episode left a legacy of bad feeling among the members of the respective organisations, spurred on by arguments as to who actually owned Ede House, the local headquarters. The Trades Council, which became one of the most radical in the Region, took the lead in organising Council tenant opposition to the rent increase.

Campaigning for the local elections, due to be held on 4 May 1972, began in earnest as Labour hoped to continue its impressive gains in areas like Horsley Hill, Cleadon Park, Victoria and Tyne Dock. The local election leaflets, designed by the Party Agent, Marsden Councillor Jim Doneghan, still causes some latter-day disagreements as to what it actually contained. Some commentators like Mike Peel and Malcolm Campbell argue that the leaflet included a definite commitment not to implement the Rent Bill if the Labour Party was returned to power. Jim Florence on the other hand maintains that it merely mentioned the Party's opposition to the Rent Bill. The man who actually designed the leaflet, Jim Doneghan, also maintains that there was no specific promise.

Despite what either side claims, all agree that the issue of implementation/non-implementation played only a minor part in the election campaign. Other issues, notably the Progressive Council's record in council house sales, land sales and the Council's decision to sell a prestigious site next to the local College to a private developer rather than build a much needed leisure centre seem to have played a more significant role.

Inspection of the Shields Gazette letters page (always a good indication of what the public feels important) also reveals that the Rent Bill issue played a very small part in the overall campaign.

The Progressives went into the election under the slogan 'Three years of Progress', proudly announcing that there had been no rent increase for two years. 'Don't forget the bad old days under Labour', the leaflet concluded.[31] However, in the face of voter dissatisfaction with the national Government, the Progressives could not expect to retain control. In all, they lost eight seats, the Labour Party had victories where in the past they only dreamed of success. Bents, Cleadon Park, Victoria, all fell to the Labour candidates, and in some cases the Labour majority was over 500.

The Housing Chair, George Smith, chose not to re-contest his Tyne Dock seat since he had decided to seek election in 1973 to the new Tyne and Wear County Council. Meanwhile, the new Housing Chairman, Billy Malcolm went straight to the Town Hall and advised Officials not

HARTON WARD

ALL TENANTS - -

YOUR RENT IS GOING UP

Say No (with your vote) to the Tories unfair rents bill.

There is no justice in it for you

A Labour Councillor **will fight** the bill.

PENSIONERS' BUS PASS
SCHOOL FARES

Progressive Councillors said **NO** to cheaper fares for
Pensioners and Schoolchildren. Labour **will** say **YES**.

COUNCIL RENTS

At the Town Council meeting on 1st March, 1972 Labour
said three rent free weeks to all Council tenants.

ALL Progressive Councillors present voted **NO**

VOTE LABOUR

McKAY - - X

Published by Jim Doneghan, 143 Westoe Road, South Shields, and
Printed by F. & A. Tolson, Ltd., Bede Industrial Estate, Jarrow.

to allow any further sales of Council houses except those already being considered (in line with the policy of the local Party).[32]

After three years out of power, the local Labour Party was back in the driving seat.

The more astute elderly Labour Councillors and Aldermen, must have wished that they had not gained the required seats for victory, for whilst they were prepared to play the non-implementation card in public for the sake of the elections, in private they were becoming deeply concerned about their Party's continued commitment to the non-implementation of the Rent Bill.

20

Chapter 2

Local Opposition to
the new Legislation

What's that sound of fairy feet? It's landlords dancing in the street;
The Champagne pops, they gorge and swill, thanks to Walker's
Housing Bill!

Major Sam Waldman [1]

On the night of Tuesday 27 June 1972, over 100 tenants, Councillors and trade unionists crowded into the Middle Club, Victoria Road, to formulate their campaign against the Rent Bill which was still making its way through Parliament.[2]

The Meeting had been organised by the Trades Council principally through its left-wing Secretary, Jack Grassby, who asked the new Chairman of the Housing Committee, Billy Malcolm, to address the meeting. Flushed with the scale of Labour's success in the local elections, which took every one by surprise, the public meeting was in defiant mood and agreed unanimously that if the Rent Bill became Law then they would all go on rent strike rather than pay any increase.

The meeting also formally agreed to contact the ruling Labour Group on the Council to request that they stand by their previous pledges not to implement the Bill if it became Law. The Housing Chairman assured the tenants that they had his support and that he would resign as Housing Chairman before being party to mass evictions of Council tenants if there was a rent strike. Jack Grassby defiantly told the meeting that it was only through direct action of the kind taken by the miners, Liverpool dockers and railway workers that they would secure victory for their cause.

Grassby occupies an interesting role in the rent issue. Affectionately known as 'Peter Pan' for his youthful looks, he became the first Secretary

21

of the Trades Council following its separation from the Labour Party in 1970. Always a radical he was a mysterious figure to many Labour Party stalwarts. He introduced to South Shields a left-wing campaigning style that it had never witnessed before and successfully developed a new style of politics in the Trades Council.

Jack Grassby

His aim was to create an alternative power centre to the establishment, whether the establishment was the Local Council or the Labour Party. As a result the Trades Council allowed into its ranks 'Associate Members' — such as pensioners organisations; student bodies; the Claimants Union and the unemployed — in addition to the affiliation of local Trades Unions. Although they could not vote, these 'social members' were a valuable element in developing the political philosophy of the Trades Council — Direct Action.

In this work, Grassby was assisted by Joe Slevin, a South Shields-born radical who became a founder of the National Claimants Union. Slevin returned to the town in the late 1960s and was to prove an effective conduit to Grassby's grassroots work during the rent strike.

Grassby and Slevin were the driving force behind many of the Trades Council's well publicised campaigns, in particular the campaign in which the local college was encouraged to run courses for unemployed people in receipt of benefit for 21 hours or six half-days a week.

Mike Peel, who at the time was the Trades Council's Assistant Secretary, believes that this was probably the most successful campaign ever launched by the Trades Council and yet he feels it was very much under-rated. The Campaign, he recalls, saw some good co-operation between the local MP, Arthur Blenkinsop and the Trades Council.

But it was Grassby's leaflet, 'A school leaver's guide to survival', which caused the most controversy. It nearly resulted in Grassby losing his employment as a college lecturer and gained national prominence. The leaflet was overtly Marxist since it warned young people of the perils of capitalism with its thirst for profit. The Daily Telegraph ran an article entitled 'Full Marx'. The Labour Party disowned the leaflet, the Town Council publicly condemned it and the College hierarchy interviewed Grassby over it.

And yet Grassby was a mystery to Labour Party traditionalists. Despite never seeking elected office, he seemed to guide the Labour Group's opposition to the Rent Bill 'from the outside looking in'. In this he was assisted by people loyal to the Trades Council, notable among them Malcolm Campbell, a Councillor for Rekendyke, and many observers believe Grassby's 'eyes and ears in the Group'. Needless to say the Council Leadership deeply resented Grassby because they could never be certain where he stood politically. Latter-day commentators have even gone as far as to say he was actively seeking to take over the South Shields Labour Party by mass infiltration of extremist elements, although Grassby today strongly denies such claims. The allegations remain unproved, but nevertheless there were attempts to suspend and even expel him from the Labour Party.

It is fascinating to speculate that had Grassby not been active politically, then the Rent Bill may not have been as fervently opposed in South Shields.

The following evening, the Shields Gazette's official line was that any rent strike would be illegal. It claimed that the Trades Council was 'whipping-up' opposition against the Rent Bill. The newspaper ended with the stirring words:

> In a democracy decisions of Parliament must be accepted since the alternative is anarchy.[3]

It was clear that no support for a rent strike would be forthcoming from the fourth estate.

Undeterred, the Trades Council resolved to set up a Housing

sub-committee under the Chairmanship of Jim Riddle, a self confessed 'conservative' Communist and member of the National Union of Tailor and Garment Workers Union. Riddle was responsible for organising meetings on the Council estates with the aim of setting up active Tenants Associations. Such Associations were already established on the Woodbine, West Harton and Victoria estates, and the principal aim was to ensure the support of tenants for rent strike (should one become necessary) and to maintain pressure on the local Councillors.

Riddle was to prove an able lieutenant to Grassby. Outside of South Shields, he rose to become an elected lay official for the Tailor and Garment Workers Union. Horrified at the election of a Communist, the Union's national leadership sent him to Northern Ireland as the Union's convenor. Meeting workers in a Belfast factory, he was asked, "Are you a Protestant or a Catholic?", to which he replied, "Neither, I'm a communist". He was immediately accepted by the workforce and was able to succeed in defending the interests of trade unionists wherever he felt there was injustice.[4]

The Labour Party privately viewed the establishment of the Tenants Associations with deep suspicion, although some Councillors **did** participate in them (in particular Albert Elliott in Whiteleas) and even held officerships in them. Jim Riddle recalls that the idea was also to ensure that the local Councillors felt that they were not alone and thus encourage them to continue to support the non-implementation line in the Council Chamber.

While the Trades Council sought to build the barricades, in the Labour Party camp disagreements were beginning to emerge. Prominent in these were Jim Doneghan, the Council's Education Committee Chairman, and Murtagh and Liz Diamond, husband and wife team from the Brinkburn Ward.

Liz Diamond argues that both Murtagh and herself were always unhappy at the way the South Shields Labour Party had committed itself to back non-implementation of the Rent Bill. If the Bill became the Law of the land, then that should be the end of the matter — laws had to be obeyed.[5]

Doneghan is more forthright, arguing that no tenant would attempt to bail the Councillors out if they were surcharged for not implementing the Bill. Indeed he recalls one argument with Jack Grassby, an owner-occupier, in which he said that if Grassby sold his house and donated the proceeds to a fighting fund then Doneghan would vote against implementation. "It was a game," claims Doneghan, "in which some people simply did not appreciate the full consequences of their actions."[6]

These comments demonstrate that as early as June 1972, just weeks after the Council elections, disagreements were emerging about the course of action being taken; indeed in an article one month before the Council elections, Alderman

'Break your pledge' call to Labour

By Malcom Scott, Our Municipal Reporter

SOUTH SHIELDS Labour Party is being urged to go back on its pre-election promise that it would defy the Government's "fair rents" Bill.

Ald. Ernest Mackley, leader of the controlling Labour group on the council, revealed today that he is calling on his colleagues to implement the Bill after all when it becomes law.

He denied that this was an "about-face" in policy. He claimed a loophole in the Bill could be used to establish South Shields as

Ald. Ernest Mackley, Labour group leader, who denies that his move is an "about-face" on the Fair Rents Bill. "We will not lead a rent strike," he says.

Mackley clearly stated that a rent rise of £1 a week would be needed in October because of the Progressives' refusal to raise them earlier.

Grassby was always suspicious of the Labour Party's actions: "There was never any doubt in my mind that they would implement the Bill if it became law. I think we all suspected they would".[7]

Meanwhile, the Labour Party's National Executive Committee urged Labour Authorities not to break the law. At a specially convened Labour Party Conference in London on Saturday 8 July over 150 representatives heard Anthony Crosland MP, Labour's Housing Spokesman, warn that the national Party would not support any Labour Council refusing to implement the Rent Bill if it became law. Instead, Crosland urged Labour Councillors to operate a three-point programme on the Rent Bill. Firstly, to undertake a campaign to try and prevent the Bill becoming law, secondly, use every legal loophole to protect Council tenants and finally, to pin responsibility for any rent rises on the Conservative Government.[8]

The Government had already agreed changes to the Bill following representations from Birmingham, Newcastle and Hammersmith Councils, which in effect meant that they could implement a smaller rent increase than that demanded by the Government as a result of their rents being already higher than in some urban areas.

Ald. E. Mackley
Photo: South Tyneside Libraries

Mackley attended the meeting on behalf of the Labour Group and upon returning home issued a press statement on the 12th July stating that he would be calling upon his colleagues to break their previous pledges and implement the Bill if it became law. Mackley argued that a loophole in the Bill could be used to declare South Shields a special area because of the high unemployment and high number of pensioners. [9]

Mackley may have also been testing the water to see what the reaction of his Labour colleagues would be to his statement because he may have begun to have his own doubts about the non-implementation strategy. He received a sharp rebuff from his colleagues.

Bob Growcott, the Secretary of the South Shields Labour Party, publicly described Mackley's statement as "completely unconstitutional", informing the press that on his way to work that morning Growcott was nearly thrown off the Freda Cunningham Ferry. Growcott called for Mackley's resignation as Council Leader and said that the Party had made its position clear at its Management Meeting in April.[10]

He told the Gazette newspaper, "If there is any move away at all from the Party's position, I would seriously have to review my position — and even go as far as to resign from the Party".

The Progressives, meanwhile, endeavoured to gain political mileage by saying any reversal by Labour or its non-implementation strategy would be an 'about face'.

At a special meeting of the South Shields Labour Group and the Constituency Executive Committee held on 14 July in the Town Hall, Mackley faced a barrage of criticism from angry Labour politicians. A motion of no confidence in Mackley's Leadership was moved and seconded, but he survived by a small majority. The Party reaffirmed its April decision not to implement the Housing Finance Bill if it became law.[11]

The May local elections had resulted in a shift in the balance of power on the national Association of Municipal Councils (AMC). Jarrow Labour Councillor Peter Hepburn succeeded in persuading the AMC to remit a previous resolution 'welcoming' the Fair Rents Bill, which had been approved during Tory domination of the Association. Speaking at the Association's meeting in London, Hepburn said:

> At £12 a week for a Council house, one could probably buy a house much cheaper. The AMC should put on record the fact that this interference with local Government has got to stop.[12]

Meanwhile, with the directive from the Labour Group in place, Councillors attended a special meeting of the Housing Committee held on 24 July. The meeting had been convened to determine whether the Authority should take advantage of the so-called 'Birmingham Clause'.

Alan Stansfield, the Council's Deputy Town Clerk, was careful to inform the meeting of the default powers contained in the Bill. Not only might it result in a Housing Commissioner being brought into the Town, but Councillors could also be surcharged and disqualified from office. Housing subsidies to the town could also be cut off by the central Government.

The Progressives argued that the Council should aim to have the Town declared a special zone under the 'Birmingham Clause' of the Bill. This stated that Councils, in certain circumstances, could make rent increases of under £1 a week. Their Labour counterparts said that this was merely a political gesture by the Progressives since the Birmingham Clause aimed to benefit the bigger cities and those Council properties recently constructed. Brinkburn's Albert Elliott proposed that no such attempts should be submitted to the Government and that the Bill would not be implemented in the Town. Any decisions of Council inconsistent with that should be amended, concluded Elliott. The motion was carried.

Billy Malcolm announced from the Chair that the Council would not be implementing the Housing Finance Bill if it became law — the decision was 'final'.[13]

This was the first time that the Council had agreed officially not to implement the Bill if it became Law. The Gazette described the decision as 'inconsistent'. In an editorial they said:

> *Has it occurred to our Labour Councillors that among the people they represent there are many thousands of law-abiding citizens who object to anyone breaking the law never mind those in office who are supposed to uphold it?*[14]

The following evening, at a special meeting of the Trades Council Executive Committee, delegates agreed a motion welcoming the Labour Party's decision not to implement the Rent Act. In addition, members agreed to contact their affiliates and request their support for any Labour Councillor subjected to a financial penalty as a result of the defiance.[15]

The Trades Council spent the summer recess of 1972 preparing its campaign to oppose the Rent Bill. Jim Riddle, Chair of the Trades Council Housing Committee, worked to establish a Tenants Association on every major Council estate.

Meanwhile the Bill formally received Royal Assent on 27 July.

The Council's ruling Labour Group met on the 10 August to determine whether they should obstruct Council Officers in exercising their new powers under the Act. The debate was rowdy and painful, and nearly a third of the Group members were absent due to summer holidays. Protests were made that the meeting should be held at a later date but were flatly rejected by the leadership, who also refused to accept a letter of 'proxy' from one Councillor who was on holiday at the time.

A motion was proposed reaffirming the Council's decision not to implement the new Act. An amendment to this was proposed by the Leadership that the Authority would not obstruct the

ENTS DECISION SPLITS LABOUR

By Our Municipal Reporter

THE Labour group on South Shields town council has decided by one vote not to stand in the way of officials preparing for the introduction of "fair rents". The vote of 13-12 represented a "slight shift" away from opposition to the Housing Finance Act, said one councillor today. But the other group members

Officers in carrying out their statutory duties under the Act. The amendment was carried by 13 votes to 12. One observer at the meeting is quoted as saying, 'all hell broke loose', with shouts of 'betrayal' and 'collaborators' by the hard-line non-implementation Councillors at those who had supported the Leadership amendment.[16]

The 12 Councillors opposed to the amendment threatened to resign the Labour Whip in order to ensure that the Council's defiance of the Act was maintained. The episode left a bad taste in the mouths of many observers because it signified a weakening of resolve by the senior Councillors and demonstrated a major policy shift in Labour's ranks. It was becoming clear that Mackley and his senior supporters were wavering in their determination to oppose the Act.

For the Progressive opposition the position was becoming so serious that they demanded an emergency Council meeting.

Stan Smith told the Gazette:

> *If the Labour Party is so divided over this issue that they are thinking of breaking the law, the proper thing to do would be to call an emergency meeting of the Town Council, so that the tenants and the community know where they stand, and perhaps more importantly, the Council Officials know what their instructions are.*[17]

Waiting until the October 4 Council meeting was unacceptable, Smith made clear an emergency meeting should be held.

Cllr. Billy Malcolm
Photo: Shields Gazette

Mackley dismissed the call for a special meeting and maintained that the Management Board had full powers of Council during the August recess.

The Council's powerful Management Board met on 14th August and formerly ratified the ruling groups decision not to obstruct the officials. It also instructed the officers to write to the Secretary of State, Peter Walker, advising that South Shields would not implement the Act, and suggested that the Government should appoint a Commissioner to undertake the task.[18]

Billy Malcolm recalled that the senior Councillors had ruled out calling a special Council meeting.

Privately, there was a feeling amongst the senior members that we were protecting the Labour Group in making the decision ourselves. If the Council supported the stance of the Board at their meeting in October, then we hoped that the District Auditor would only punish the Labour members of the Management Board. The Bill had only just become law and there was no requirement to raise any rents until October — so we felt we had some room for manoeuvre. We were obviously still very optimistic that other North East Councils would remain firm.[19]

Issuing a statement to the press, Ald Mackley, the Council Leader, said:

It is the unanimous decision of the Management Board that the Act be not implemented; that any resolutions to the contrary be rescinded and that Council officials be not obstructed in the performance of their duties under the Act.[20]

The Trades Council activists were outraged by the decision. An urgent Executive Committee was convened at which the Secretary was asked to write to Bob Growcott, the Labour Party Secretary, demanding talks over the Group's decision.

Grassby wrote:

> *We believe the logic of the Labour Group's original decision to refuse to implement the Rent Act because of its unjust character leads to the conclusion that it would be hypocritical to assist with its administration or to collaborate with any Government administration agent.*
>
> *The Labour Group's decision could well mean that the Labour Party is accused of collaboration with the Tory Rent Commissioner and a betrayal of its re-election pledge.*
>
> *The Executive feels that for such an important policy decision to be taken, all the Labour Councillors should have the opportunity to be present.*
>
> *We call upon the South Shields Labour Party to exert its maximum influence with the Labour Group to ensure that it returns to its former commitment for vigorous opposition to the Rent Act.* [21]

There were suspicions among the Trades Council's activists that the Council Leadership had deliberately arranged for the Group to be held in August (when the Authority is traditionally in recess) knowing that at least 25 members would be unable to attend. One hard-line Labour Group member had endeavoured to vote by proxy when realising he would be unable to attend the crucial Group meeting.

A. D. Maxwell, who had recently moved to Cambridge but still maintained a keen interest in local affairs, also echoed these suspicions. Maxwell, in one of the few letters to appear in the Shields Gazette on the Rent Act issue, wrote:

> *I read that Ald Mackley and his colleagues decided to let the officers make a start on something they don't intend shall ever be carried out. Either this is a waste of time and money or the Alderman secretly intends that Shields will put the Bill into operation. I wonder why he had the latest Group meeting at a time when his opponents in his Group were away? It seems very suspicious.* [22]

Meanwhile, Growcott had no personal objections to convening an emergency meeting of the South Shields Labour Party, but he would only have been able to do so with the permission of the Party Chairman, Murtagh Diamond — now a staunch opponent of the non-implementation policy. Diamond, determined that the Party should begin to distance itself from the rebels, agreed to the request and the special Executive meeting was convened for 25 August — the Trades Council would not be invited.[23]

Grassby and his Trades Council colleagues had begun to realise that with the Labour Party operating a 'Janus Head' approach to the Rent Act, they would need to step up their campaign to mobilise mass popular support against the Act. On the 17 August Whiteleas was to host a public meeting with the aim of establishing a Tenants Association. It became the scene of one of the biggest public meetings held in South Shields during the Rent Act issue.[24]

Nearly five hundred residents crowded into St. Oswald's Church Hall and heard the Chairman of the Housing Committee, Billy Malcolm, describe the effects of the new Act if it were implemented. He said that the Act was the most vicious piece of class legislation since the war. However, whilst he informed residents that it was still Labour Party policy to oppose the Rent Act, tenants would need to give Councillors strong support if they were going to continue travelling down that non-implementation road.

Albert Elliott was elected the Tenants Associations Secretary and pledged to the tenants that he would continue to oppose the Act even if it meant going to prison. Elliott, a Councillor for the neighbouring Brinkburn Ward, lived in Whiteleas and had long coveted a seat representing his home ward. With this in mind, he is quoted in the Gazette as having demanded the Whiteleas Councillors attend the next Tenants Associations meeting to explain where they stood on the Rent Act issue.

Grassby gave an eloquent speech claiming that if only five Councillors were sent to prison they would have struck a blow against the Act. He also mischievously suggested that all Labour Councillors should resign and 'go to the people' on the issue.[25]

Local tenants suggested that the Council should hold a referendum on whether to implement the Rent Act (an interesting suggestion considering that today, Local Councils are encouraged to undertake such initiatives by central Government).

But even on the issue of the establishment of Tenants Associations there was hostility between the Labour Party and the Trades Council. On the 23 August the Trade Council felt it necessary to issue a public statement instructing Labour Councillors to 'resist the temptation' to take over the Tenants Association. Grassby claimed that

Cllr. Albert Elliott
Photo: Shields Gazette

'manipulation' by the Labour Party had nearly resulted in one of the Associations splitting, but he refused to reveal which one.[26]

The main aim of the Associations was to prepare for a rent strike when the Act was finally implemented in South Shields. As a consequence many Councillors viewed them with distrust. Jim Doneghan said that if the Associations were 'genuine' then they would have been concerned at improving their communities and quality of life.[27]

Grassby maintains that the Associations, in time, would have become more than merely Rent Strike agencies. Once the Trades Council had established an Association with the use of 'flying squads' which undertook the spadework, they would be independent, democratic bodies dealing with a wide range of issues in their local communities.[28]

Within two weeks a further Association was set up in Cleadon Park with over 150 tenants joining. Tenants Associations now existed on the

Woodbine, Victoria and Whiteleas housing estates. Grassby announced that all the Tenants Associations in the town would unite under the banner of 'South Shields Federation of Tenants Associations'.

Meanwhile the National Union of Public Employees (NUPE) took steps nationally to protect its members. Their National Executive agreed that any members who worked for a 'rebel' Authority refusing to operate the Housing Finance Act would receive the support of the Union if they supported the policies of the Council in the course of their work duties.

Locally, Labour's Executive Committee met in emergency session on 25 August to discuss Grassby's letter. The Executive agreed to hold a meeting of the full Management Committee with a motion from the Executive supporting the Group's decision not to obstruct the Council Officials.

The meeting was scheduled for 31 August. Two days prior to this, a further row erupted between the Party and the Trades Council. This time, Jim Davison, a Councillor in the predominately Council house ward of Biddick Hall, accused the Trades Council of sabotaging his public meeting by calling a rival meeting before his own. The approaches though were different. Davison wanted a meeting to explain to the tenants what was happening and his own views in relation to the Act, the Trades Council obviously wanted a meeting to establish a Biddick Hall Tenants Association, in line with its published policy, Davison reluctantly called off his own meeting. [29]

Cllr. Jim Davison
Photo: Shields Gazette

Davison's own role in the rent issue is interesting. Utterly sincere in his opposition to the Act, he nevertheless genuinely objected to the principle of a rent strike. Such a policy, he felt, would place the very roofs over the heads of Council tenants in jeopardy.

The Trades Council continued with its

meeting and on the 30 August 1972 the sixth Tenants Association was duly formed in Biddick Hall.[30]

Labour's Management Committee — at which the Trades Council were not formally invited — voted heavily in favour of the Executive Committee recommendation to the support the Labour Group's decision in relation to the Council Officers. The vote was 39 – 3, which suggests that some very intense 'behind the scenes' lobbying was being undertaken within Labour's ranks to prepare for an ultimate 'U-turn' in the non-implementation strategy.[31]

Mackley advised the Gazette newspaper that the local Party would set up a liaison committee with the local Trades Union Council to publicise the full effects of the Act as far as tenants were concerned. Grassby said at the time that he believed that such a co-ordinated front of the Labour Party, tenants and Trades Council would "…kill the Act in South Shields".[32]

Delegates attending the 31 August Labour Party Management Committee meeting at the Armstrong Hall in Stanhope Road would have gone along knowing that in the previous night Wallsend Council had agreed unanimously to reverse its previous decision of non-implementation to the Rent Act. Alderman Mali described the Act as, "…the worst piece of anti-working class legislation ever perpetrated on the backs of the workers in the last 40 years".[33]

His colleague, Ald. T. Black, said that he had been disheartened that he had yet to hear the first bleep against the Act from the tenants themselves. It appeared to Ald. Black that the tenants were not concerned about their own conditions.[34]

On the 30 August, Felling UDC had also met and voted to rescind its previous resolution — "All Council tenants are already paying fair rents and therefore no increase will be necessary on 1 October".[35]

Whilst South Shields maintained defiance (of some kind), their Labour Council colleagues in Jarrow were meeting in the same evening and voting to implement the Act. Don Dixon, the Council's Finance

Chairman, told the Gazette that it was always the Labour Council's intention to implement the Act once it had become law.

Sunderland Council also met in emergency session on the 31 August following a notice of motion from five Authority members (Councillors Slater, Lewins, Waistell, Heatle and Dodds). Their resolution read:

(1) That minute 5(E) of the Report of the Housing Committee of the Council at its meeting on 12 January and which was adopted by the Council be rescinded.

(2) That pursuant to the provisions of the Housing Finance Act 1972, this Council resolves that the present rents of all Council dwellings are 'fair rents' and that as a consequence thereof pursuant to section 62 (4), the Secretary of State be invited to direct the Council there is no need for an increase in rents in the year 1972/73.[36]

The rebellion was short-lived; the Authority voted 43-18 to implement the Act following a decision by the Labour Group on the Authority to retract its earlier opposition.

Meanwhile, on Tyneside, Gateshead Council's General Purposes Committee approved a report on the same night instructing the Officers to implement the Act on the Council's 14,000 tenants, once the full Council had approved the Committee's recommendation. [37]

Neighbouring Hebburn Urban District Council agreed to implement the new Act on Friday 1 September. Hugh Downey, a senior Hebburn Councillor, described it as "the worst night in our lives". They agreed to raise the rents of their tenants by 55p per week. Councillor Neil Bonnar said, "It was abhorrent to Councillors that a commissioner might be able to take over the administration of housing in Hebburn".[38]

Letters to Hebburn's Council tenants would end with the words:

Your Council will continue to oppose the Housing Finance Act and looks forward to the day when this vindictive legislation is removed from the statute book.

Today, Neil Bonnar maintains that there was never any real likelihood of Northern Councils opposing the Tory Government over the Fair Rents issue:

> *The initial reactions to the proposals were that they were outrageous and had to be opposed, but there was no question that Labour Councils in the Region would vote to implement the proposals if the Bill became Law. It simply wasn't the style of politics in the North to defy the Law.*[39]

Five days later on the 6 September, the entire Labour Group on Newcastle City Council voted not to implement the Act — but they were not in control of the Authority. The Act was implemented by 35 votes to 27.[40]

Councillor Jeremy Beecham said that power for fixing the rent levels had been taken away from local Councils and vested in a Scrutiny Committee chosen by the Secretary of State for the Environment. [41]

The following evening Whickham UDC voted to implement the Rent Act.[42]

The omens were not good for the rebellion in South Shields. The Labour Council was increasingly becoming isolated in the Region, as Councils who had previously expressed opposition to the Rent Act were implementing its recommendations. The Trades Council urged calm amongst its supporters.

In a sign of things to come, the liaison committee proposed by Mackley at Labour's monthly Management Committee was never established.

But it was not just Council tenants who faced rent rises under the new Act. The 648 North-Eastern Housing Association Tenants in South Shields were aghast to find that their rents had increased £1 per week and made a formal approach to the Trades Council for assistance in the possible rent strike.[43]

Jim Riddle, as the Trades Council co-ordinator of the Tenants Association, met with each Tenants Association on a regular basis to discuss tactics. Tenants were encouraged to save money in a fighting fund in order to meet any costs that might be necessary in the future; they were also instructed that should the Council implement the Act, they should only pay the rent minus any increase.

Again, it is surprising that the Shields Gazette letters page did not contain correspondence from tenants over this issue. Indeed, the minutes of the 5 September meeting of the Labour's Party's Management Committee do not even recall the issue being discussed.[44]

Considering that half of the Labour Group were openly adopting a hard-line stance on non-implementation and even faced prison sentences for their stubbornness, it is astonishing that the Labour Party was not in negotiations with the residents to discuss tactics. This, it seems, was left to their more left-wing counterparts in the Trades Council.

The Council's Management Board met again on 27 September where a letter from Peter Walker, the Secretary of State, was submitted. (Appendix 2)

Walker was adamant that Local Authorities, as creations of Statute, were unable to pick and choose which National Legislation to implement. '...A Local Authority who decided not to perform a duty imposed by the Act are not choosing between two policies which they are free to adopt. They are choosing to act unlawfully instead of lawfully.' Walker also explained that he would **not** send a Commissioner into South Shields until the Authority was in default (had run up huge debts). The Minister also insisted that Councillors would be surcharged for any debts, would be removed from public office and might even face a prison sentence.

The Minister suggested that the Authority had made its previous decision based upon a misunderstanding of the legal position. Mackley derided this and said that he and his colleagues fully appreciated the consequences of their actions. His Progressive counterpart Stan Smith said, "I think Labour made an irresponsible election pledge; to get out of it they should eat humble pie and obey the law".

The Minister ended his letter to the Management Board with the sentence: "I hope that in view of the explanation of the legal position set out above, your Council will reconsider the resolution which you quoted in you letter".

With the 2 October deadline fast approaching — the date by which the Council must increase the rents — the Board remained unrepentant. Once again it announced that it would not implement the Act (although technically, the Labour Leadership would not have been able to recommend anything else until the Labour Group had met in full to discuss Walker's letter).

The Labour Group was scheduled to meet on 2 October, two days before the full Council, and would make a final decision on the Rent issue at that meeting.

Ken Reid, at the time a Councillor for Cleadon Park, recalls that he was quite prepared to continue voting against implementation. His main reason for rejecting this course of action was the fact that the Council had been informed that a Commissioner would only be sent into the town **after** the Councillors were in default and in debt. He believes that the Council Leadership had taken the view that they would be allowed to wash their hands of the issue and allow a Government appointee to implement the Act in town. When it became clear that this would not happen until the Authority was in financial crisis, Reid believes realism set in — 'chaos would have been the result and that would have been to the benefit of no one'.[45]

As the drama unfolded, Stan Smith, the opposition Leader, met with the Town Clerk to ensure that none of the Progressive Councillors would be held responsible if the Labour members refused to increase the rents.[46]

On the evening of the 27 September, Gateshead Council endorsed the previous decision of its General Purposes Committee and agreed to implement rent increases of 75p per week. The Labour Group had been locked behind closed doors in a bitter row over the decision, but the rent increase would go ahead.[47]

On Sunday 1 October, a mass meeting was again held in South Shields, this time in the Bolingbroke Hall. The meeting pledged support to the North Eastern Housing Association Tenants who were refusing to pay the £1 increase in their rents and agreed a five-point position put forward by Jim Riddle.

These points were:
1. Formally record opposition by the Federation to the Housing Finance Act.
2. To give every kind of help to the North Eastern Housing Association Tenants.

3. To launch petitions in the town and, led by jazz bands, to parade to the Town Hall to present the petitions to the Mayor, Vincent Fitzpatrick
4. To express appreciation to the Labour Group for refusing to implement the Act
5. To rally at the Town Hall on Wednesday evening to show disapproval of the Rent Act.

The meeting was well attended. Over 600 tenants gave Riddle loud applause when he called upon any Labour Councillors having second thoughts about the Rent Act to resign before Wednesday evening's Council meeting to ensure that they did not betray themselves or the ward they represented.[48]

The Mayor attended the meeting in an unofficial capacity and told the tenants only to refuse to pay the increase in rent. It would, he advised, be the Council in default not the tenants. Grassby again stated that a rent strike would defeat the Rent Act. He informed the meeting that the Trades Council would seek a national strike if any tenant or Councillor were threatened.

Absent from the meeting were Billy Malcolm and Doug Ridley, the Chair and Vice Chair of the Housing Committee. They were both at a Housing Conference in Scarborough, at which high on the agenda would be the Housing Finance Act. Malcolm recalls that he was still of the opinion that the Council should refuse to implement the Act and both he and Ridley intended to return early from the conference to vote in the crucial meeting to be held on Wednesday evening.[49]

On Monday 2 October, the Council had begun running up its first debt under the new Act, to the sum of £16,000 per week. South Shields was one of only 17 local authorities in the Country still refusing to raise the rents.

The Shields Gazette, who had made its own opposition to the Council stance clear on so many occasions, helpfully reminded the Labour members that refusing to implement the Act could result in their being surcharged and disqualified from office for five years. They also advised that any rebel Councillor who refused to increase the rents ran the risk of sharing the bill for any losses incurred.

That evening's Labour Group meeting was bitter and divisive. Doneghan, Murtagh and Liz Diamond, Ken Webster and his mother Vi, all made it clear to the Group that they were not prepared to either stand alone or break the law.

At the meeting Mackley, who was also Chair of the Labour Group, suggested that all members should be given a free vote on the issue in the Chamber so that Labour Councillors could vote according to their conscience and not as a political group.[50]

Cllr. Jim Doneghan
Photo: Shields Gazette

On this compromise, the position becomes confusing. Davison, a staunch opponent of Act, voted **for** a free vote since he believed that the Group had no right to enforce its will on individual members when the issue was so sensitive.[51] Doneghan on the other hand, a staunch opponent of the non-implementation strategy, voted **against** a free vote since he claims Councillors supporting non-implementation wanted to grant a free vote knowing people like himself would vote in favour of implementation and in effect 'get the rebels off the hook'. It was a disgraceful tactic, he claimed:

>...it would have amounted to me cutting my own throat, since those who would allow us a free vote in the Chamber, would then call us betrayers when the Act was implemented — I do not believe they had any intention whatsoever of not implementing the Act, they merely wanted others to do the dirty deed for them. [52]

If that was the ploy, then it was certainly clever. Mackley urged his colleagues to adopt the policy. Labour's majority on the Council was 14 and it was evident that a huge split had developed in the Labour ranks. Allowing a free vote would enable those opposed to breaking the Law to vote in favour of implementation. These 'new' Labour rebels, together with the Progressive Councillors, would ensure the Act's implementation. For Mackley, it would mean that the Labour Group could still claim to be opposed to the implementation of the Act and then blame the subsequent rent increase on both those Labour members who rebelled and the Progressive Association.

Doneghan recalls that the debate was spiteful and vindictive — the vote in the Group being 17-15 in favour of granting a free vote. The Trades Council immediately realised the implications of the free vote and announced that it was a betrayal of the election pledge made in May.

Jack Grassby realised that with a free vote, the chances of the Council voting in favour of non-implementation were minimal. Doneghan himself, when interviewed in 1989, still felt bitter about the free vote decision, since he felt that the Group Leadership had used both himself and other Labour Councillors who had voted for implementation of the Act as scapegoats. Indeed, he says that he approached the Progressive Leader, Stan Smith, and jokingly suggested that the Progressive Councillors should stay away from the crucial Council meeting — 'that would have shook them!' said Doneghan.[53]

Rekendyke Councillor Dickie Barry voted against granting a free vote, believing that the Group should have shown a united front. But he was realistic to know the tactics behind the decision.

> It was clear that once the free vote was granted, the fight was over. There was clearly a number of Labour councillors deeply unhappy with the non-implementation strategy, the Diamonds, Doneghan, Jordison and the Websters. Their votes alone with a couple of abstentions would have resulted in the Act's implementation.[54]

Stan Smith described the 'Free vote' decision as the 'first sign of sanity, which has been visible this year'. He concluded his comments to the Gazette by saying, 'I think members of the Council have been egged on by those reactionary elements in the South Shields Trades Council'.[55]

The years have not mellowed Stan Smith's original thoughts. Today he maintains that there was never any question of the Progressive Group not implementing the Law.

In principle we accepted the Housing Act although it was not popular. I think that some of the more senior Councillors in the Labour Party accepted that they should obey the law of the land. Some of them were JPs; they had homes, families and jobs. There was no reason to give all that up at the request of a bunch of communists and their friends fishing in troubled waters.[56]

With the Labour Group hopelessly split, the Trades Council and their Tenants Association satellites appeared to be the sole bastion of opposition to the Rent Act. They received encouragement from the Labour Party National Conference meeting in Blackpool that week. Delegates voted against their NEC Leadership in favour of a plan to compensate any rebel Councillor who was penalised financially for defiance of the new Law.

Labour's monthly Management Committee meeting was held on 3 October at the Party's headquarters in Westoe Road. Hard-line rebels like Malcolm Campbell prepared a last-ditch manoeuvre to force a show-down with the Government.

It is astonishing that the attendance at the meeting was less than 35 delegates. The local Council was on the verge of defying the law of the land with the active encouragement of the local Trades Council and Tenants Groups, yet the policy-making body of the Constituency Labour Party had one of its lowest attendances.

Following apologies for absences, Campbell moved from the floor of the meeting that, "item five, the Labour Group report be brought forward and discussed first on the Agenda". This was probably due to the fact that some of his colleagues were unable to remain for the full meeting and would need to leave early. Not surprisingly the Chairman, Murtagh Diamond, ruled against the motion and Delegates challenged the ruling, but the Chair's ruling was upheld. When Councillor Ken Scrimger finally gave the Group Report, there again followed a heated and acrimonious debate. Malcolm Campbell and Jim Davison told delegates that they would resign from the Council if the Rent Act was implemented.Hard-liners sought to enforce discipline by preventing any Councillors who voted in favour of implementation from being allowed to stand as Labour Party candidates in the future elections.

The following resolution was moved and seconded:

> *That any member of the Labour Group who votes for the implementation of the Rent Act at the Council meeting on 4 October 1972, or who cannot give good reason for not turning up at the Council meeting, be not readopted for the Metropolitan or District Council Election.*

An amendment was subsequently moved — 'That this is a short sighted policy and should not be supported' — not strictly an amendment, but obviously accepted by the Chairman of the meeting. The vote was 13 in favour of the resolution and 16 supporting the amendment.[57]

An unnamed spokesman for the Trades Council told the Gazette, "The Labour Party has passed the political initiative on to the Tories. Opposition to the Act will now come from the tenants and trade unionists".[58]

The South Shields Labour Party thus gave the green light for any members wanting to vote in favour of implementation.

Chapter 3

The Mandate for Resistance

The word reluctant must have been used in more Town Hall Council
Chambers than at any other time in their history.
Clay Cross Councillor [1]

Following the refusal by the Council Management Board on two occasions to agree to implement the Rent Act, the ball passed to the full South Shields County Borough Council to determine their course of action. The Council met on the evening of the 4 October.

Tenants crowded into the Civic Chambers public gallery whilst outside in Westoe Road and Beach Road over 500 tenants waited and cheered Labour Councillors as they entered the Town Hall. Placards, jazz bands and a police presence greeted the Councillors as they walked up the main steps into the Victorian building.

Billy Malcolm, the Housing Chairman and his Vice Chairman, Doug Ridley travelled back from a major Housing Conference in Scarborough in order to attend the proceedings and cast their votes.

Inside the Chamber, Progressive Ken Charlton opened the debate when the Management Boards recommendations of the 27 September were discussed.

Let us not be misled by the louder members of our community and change
the issue. Whatever the rights and wrongs of the Act may be, the fact that
it's Statute Law means that it must be upheld.

You have got yourselves into considerable difficulty, but we will not bail
you out. We will support any in your Party who wish to implement the
Law, but we will not propose anything.

Tenants in the public gallery jeered, to which Ken Charlton responded

"Progressive Leaders"
left to right: Ald. H. W. Abey, MBE Cllr. S. Smith, Cllr. J. McKee
Photo: Shields Gazette

by saying:

> *It is sad that the people behind you do not know how much less they could pay. It is a fact that the lower income groups get substantial help from this Act.[2]*

John Wakeford, a Labour Councillor from Biddick Hall and a local Magistrate, said his position was unchanged on the Act.

> *I will not be party to the implementation of this Act. I had hoped this line would be followed by other authorities.*

> *I will continue to oppose this Act. If a decision to implement is taken, then I shall resign as a Councillor.[3]*

John McKee, a Progressive Councillor from West Park said that a campaign had been waged in the town to incite and frighten Council tenants. Tenants were worried about increase rents, but the Act provided greater subsidies to those in the greatest need. There had been arguments against a means test, but Cllr. McKee stated that income tax itself was a means test.

46

He expressed particular concern that if the Act was not implemented then benefits would be lost and in the long term, local rates would need to increase to cover deficits run up by the Council. "If you don't like the law, work through your Party to get the Government changed", he said.[4]

Visibly shaken, Liz Diamond told the Council that deciding which way to vote had been made with intense agony, but the threat of cutting all housing subsidies would have resulted in areas of her Brinkburn ward not being modernised.

...there is no other way, I must uphold the Law. [5]

Doneghan made his way to her seat to comfort her as she was barracked from the public gallery.

Billy Malcolm described the Act as nothing less than political blackmail. The Group's decision for a free vote was a majority decision, he said, and told Council members that if they did not implement the Act then they must move from passive resistance to active resistance. The tenants, still of the opinion that he would vote against implementation, cheered, after which he replied:

I disagree with that because I believe in the Parliamentary system. It is not the Labour Party view to support rent strikes.

I will not sit back and watch as South Shields becomes a no-go area and this must be the ultimate end.

He continued:

If I thought that by going to jail tomorrow I could save this rent increase, I would readily go.

Commenting on his change of position, Malcolm argued that whilst in Scarborough at the Housing Conference, he was taken aback at the scale of opposition from other Authorities as to what South Shields was doing. Other Authorities had taken the decision to implement the Act without much public outrage. But there was another aspect that had also grieved him in Scarborough. He had spoken to London councillors who had talked him through the 1921 decision by Lansbury and the Poplar

Guardians not to increase their precept to the London County Council. It had resulted in their being jailed and surcharged.

Some of those former Councillors went to their graves in debt, I simply could not allow that to happen. If the North East Councils who had originally promised to refuse to implement had remained steadfast then we had a chance but we simply could not fight alone. We were the last Council in the North East to implement the Act, we would have maintained defiance but without the other Councils it was pointless, we couldn't have done it on our own.[6]

Sep Robinson, at the time Chairman of the Housing Committee for the Boldon UDC, remembers the Conference well and said that there was never any doubt in his mind that the Act should be obeyed.

South Shields simply could not stand alone, it was a ludicrous situation — whether or not the Labour Councillors implemented the Act did not matter, the rent increase would still go ahead, the only difference would be, the rebels would have had a massive surcharge on their head.[7]

This he told Billy Malcolm and Doug Ridley. Malcolm maintained that he was always opposed to rent strikes because he did not think them practicable.

Travelling back to South Shields for the Council meeting, both Malcolm and Ridley — still opposed to the Act — nevertheless agreed to vote in favour of its implementation in South Shields.

Doneghan gave a forceful speech that was continually interrupted by tenants in the Gallery; at one stage Grassby threw Labour Party election leaflets into the Chamber during his speech. Leaping over the partition, Grassby threw more leaflets until Progressives Jim Crawley and Jim Capstick seized him. Doneghan was the Labour Party's Agent and had designed the leaflets, which Grassby claimed gave an undertaking not to implement the Act.

Fully expecting to be arrested that evening, Grassby had ensured that his solicitor's home telephone number was in his top pocket. The Mayor ordered the public gallery to be cleared and the police moved forward to remove the tenants ,at which they began chanting, 'We shall not be moved', but they were, and after an interval of 20 minutes the Council's debate continued behind closed doors.

Doneghan continued:

> *One thing that has never been spelt out to them (the Council tenants). Whether we implement or not it does not make one ha'pence of difference in the long run.*

> *But changing society by violence rarely, if ever, brings a better system or a better society. If I had said this a few years ago, I would have laughed at myself, the idea of reds under bed. But I sincerely believe that if this Council takes one step toward active resistance it means a step towards violence. And once you get violence it is taken out of the hands of the moderates and goes to those fringe people who come out of the woodwork at such times.*

He ended by saying that if people who elected him were unhappy with the way that he voted then they would be able to replace him at the next elections.[8]

The Council Leader pleaded with the tenants not to go on a rent strike. Mackley said:

> *...by doing so they would place the very roofs over their heads in jeopardy, and that is far more important than any Tory Law or its effects.*

> *If the tenants disagree with this, they will be led up a hill and left there. And those who took them there will be powerless to help them.*

He told the Council that when the Labour Group had agreed with the non-implementation strategy it was on the strength of other local authorities also agreeing with the tactic. Now, he said, "We are out on a limb". [9]

The vote on the Management Board's recommendation was taken and resulted in its being thrown out with the help of 13 Labour Councillors siding with the Progressives. By this time, the Council had been in session for nearly three hours. Suggestions were made that the Authority should adjourn and meet on another evening to conclude business. However the Town Clerk, R. S. Young, advised Councillors that a decision had to be taken that night one way or another. Labour members then barracked the Progressives, shouting, 'It's your Act, you implement it'. When no Labour Councillor moved the necessary motion for implementation, the Progressive Housing spokesman, Jim Capstick, stood up in the Chamber and declaring:

In the absence of any responsibility from the other side...,

moved the resolution.

It was a named vote and saw the Rent Act finally implemented in South Shields by 31 votes to 22. Voting with the 20 Progressives were 11 'new' Labour rebels including Liz and Murtagh Diamond, Billy Malcolm, Doug Ridley, Ken Webster and Ken Reid. Surprisingly, Mackley voted against implementation.

Cllrs. Liz and Murtagh Diamond   *Photo: S. Tyneside Libraries*

Bob Growcott recalls being incensed at the way both Malcolm and Ridley had voted.

I worked the numbers out over the previous weekend. Malcolm and Ridley were going to a Housing Conference in Scarborough. They assured me that they would be returning to vote against implementation. We simply had no inclination that they had switched their votes. Something happened in those intervening three days to make them change their minds — no doubt about it.[10]

But Growcott accepts there were intense pressures on Councillors.

I well recall meeting my ward colleague, Vi Webster, at her home. Her husband was a police sergeant and he made it absolutely clear that if she voted to break the law he would not allow her back in the house, the same would have happened to his son Ken. Whether that would actually have happened I don't know, but it does demonstrate the pressure members were under.[11]

Billy Malcolm's quick return from Scarborough meant that he did not have the opportunity to discuss the matter with his ward colleague Dickie Barry, but today Barry would have no criticism of Malcolm.

He did what he felt was right. It was certainly the case that by the time South Shields came to make our decision, we were standing alone. Perhaps Billy, in Scarborough, realised that we could not win. Certainly, we would have been thrown out of office and surcharged for our troubles. Looking back, I can't help feeling that the whole business got out of hand, the tenants had been whipped up. But the final decision was a seven-day wonder. People got on with their lives and paid the rent increase — and Billy went on to be re-elected, despite what was said in the Middle Club![12]

The reaction of the tenants outside the Town Hall was one of disbelief to Albert Elliott, standing on the Town Hall steps shouting to the crowds that the Rebels had 'sold them down the river' and implemented the Act. As Councillors left to go home they were greeted with cries of 'scabs', 'traitors', 'bastards' and 'Rachman'. There were minor scuffles and Liz Diamond was spat at, although there were no arrests.[13]

Cllr. Malcolm Campbell

Dickie Barry recalled that there were crowds outside the Town Hall that evening and the throwing of eggs and flour at Councillors who had voted for implementation.

Liz Diamond was kicked a few times, it was quite distasteful the whole event, but tempers were running high, tenants felt very badly let down.[14]

Councillors who had voted against implementation, including Malcolm Campbell and Bob Growcott, went to the Albemarle Public House and met with the Trades Council activists to talk over what had happened.[15]

Campbell remembers today that the conversation was one of disbelief at the events in the Council Chamber,

...although I don't know why we were surprised. I think we all knew the Labour Party would back down eventually. But I was just so disappointed. My whole life has been one of fighting injustice where I see it. I just felt the Rent Act was wrong, the Rent Act was the first major attack on Council housing in Britain and I don't think it ever recovered.

Asked if it were true that some Labour Councillors were seen 'counting their fingers' to see how many of their number were voting to implement the Act and so allow them to continue their own personal defiance, Campbell responded:

...oh yes, definitely. But for me it didn't matter, they were voting against the Rent Act, that was the main issue. [16]

Malcolm Campbell told the Gazette, "Alderman Mackley is the one who is completely to blame for the result. He could have tipped the balance by not supporting a free vote in the Group".

Labour Alderman George Gibson said, 'Council house tenants have been let down — they have been left to carry the can. It's a sad day for the Labour Party in Shields'.

The Councillors were particularly incensed at Ernie Mackley for the support he had given to a free vote. Had there been no free vote by the Labour Group it is very likely that South Shields would have followed the same path as Clay Cross in Derbyshire and voted not to implement the Act. As Billy Malcolm recalls,

...If the Group decision was mandatory against implementation without the provision of a free vote, I would have voted with the Group.[17]

Shields Gazette

and Shipping Telegraph

HOME

No. 33434 (Established 1849)   Thursday, October 5, 1972   3p.

COUNCIL START MASSIVE RENTS ACTION

'Resign' pair speak out

By Malcolm Scott and Steve Levinson

Coun. John Wakeford and (below) Coun. Jim Davison, who are resigning from the council in protest.

SOUTH SHIELDS corporation officials today began work on serving 16,000 council tenants with notices of rent increases in the wake of rowdy scenes at the town hall last night.

But it will be at least six weeks before the rises take effect. And in the meantime the Finance Committee is left with the problem of finding £112,000 — the deficit that will arise because of a seven-week delay in implementing the "fair rents" Act.

The Labour Party was also counting the cost — in resignations — of the council's decision to operate the Act.

Two councillors will tonight resign from the council, and at least six others have said they will resign the Labour whip.

And in the aftermath of last night's decision — which followed a noisy display of tenants' anger, accusations of betrayal and broken election promises were directed at the Labour members who voted with the Progressives.

Eleven Labour members sided with the minority group, and three others abstained, to enable the Act to go through.

Immediate reaction from tenants associations was that

OPEN FRIDAYS AND SATURDAYS UNTIL 6.0 P.M.

Growcott recalls Mackley being a very shrewd man, who 'played the game'.

Mackley had been groomed for the Leadership by the elderly Aldermen on the Council for years. Once he had it he had every intention of holding on to it. I have no doubt he knew which councillors were likely to break ranks and vote for implementation — although I doubt he was aware that Billy Malcolm and Doug Ridley would vote to implement the Act. Realising enough Labour rebels would side with the Progressives he carefully manoeuvred his vote against implementation to protect his image.[18]

Those comments were echoed by Dickie Barry,

Mackley was a clever man, he knew what the consequences of defiance would be. I have no doubt that he had no stomach for a showdown with the Government on this issue.[19]

The following day two Councillors announced that they were resigning from the Council and six Councillors declared that they were resigning the Labour Whip: Cllrs. Malcolm Campbell, Bob Growcott, Jim Hodgson, Paddy Cain, Albert Elliott and Alderman George Gibson. Malcolm Campbell told the Gazette, 'We consider ourselves the official Labour Group.[20]

The Shields Gazette — which had remained consistent in its opposition to any refusal to implement the Law — took a dim view of the events in the Council Chamber. Claiming that the Council tenants had been 'led up the garden path' by the Labour Party's pre-election promises, its Editorial Comment nevertheless maintained that their behaviour outside the Town Hall had been 'disgusting'.

Are they pleased with the way they jeered and gibed and mobbed the men and women who have tried to be honest with their consciences and vote as they saw fit, whether for implementation or against?

The Editorial continued:

They were described as an 'unruly mob' by a councillor who voted against implementation and who has in fact resigned his seat. 'I will not accept

54

the rule of mob law', he said afterwards. Those who were involved in the hysteria would do well to ponder this criticism. So would those who help to generate this hysteria.[21]

The two Councillors who resigned, Davison and Wakeford, both represented Biddick Hall. Although latter-day commentators have recalled that Wakeford would have resigned from the Council anyway because he had recently been appointed into a new managerial job, Campbell argues that this was of no consequence, '…he made it clear he would resign and he did.' Biddick Hall was predominantly Council housing and Labour's hierarchy was concerned when it was announced that Tenants Associations representatives might contest the by-election vacancies. Growcott urged the electors of Biddick Hall to rally around Davison and Wakeford.

In announcing his resignation, Davison said:

The crowd which gathered at the Town Hall had no influence on me whatsoever. In fact their actions should have driven me the other way. They were just an unruly mob. Mob rule gets no one anywhere. Mob rule leads only to the gun, brick and the bomb. I was prepared to be put on the rack, but I will not accept the rule of mob law, their behaviour was terrible.[22]

Two days later, Growcott as Party Secretary took the lead and endeavoured to limit the electoral damage. He retracted his decision to resign the Whip, encouraged others to do so by declaring the fight was within the Labour Party and prepared for the by-elections. 'The Labour Party will contest any election with a view to winning', he declared, appalled at the threat of Tenants Associations representatives opposing the Labour Party.

In a statement to the Journal newspaper, Growcott said:

We cannot get anywhere with splinter groups in the Party. Feelings were running high and there was a lot said in the heat of the moment. I call upon all Labour Councillors to reunite, to rebuild the Labour Group and strengthen the Party. We have further battles ahead and we cannot get any constructive work done if we are split. We must prepare for the elections next year.[23]

Growcott's colleague, Jim Hodgson retracted his decision to resign the Whip, leaving only three councillors and an Alderman out in the cold.[24]

While the Trades Union Council began to put into place phase one of its operation for a Borough-wide rent strike, the local Labour Party leadership put into place its own plans to distance itself from direct action and to silence the more vocal exponents of the non-implementation strategy.

Chapter 4

The Rent Strike

I despise the bubble popularity......
Thomas Hart Benton

With the establishment of 14 Tenants Association across the town and a Federation to co-ordinate their activities, the leading lights of the Trades Council were in confident spirit. They believed that they would be able not only to call a rent strike but, unlike other areas in the North, to actually sustain it over a long period of time. Grassby's aim was to have over 1,000 tenants on strike and to maintain this defiance until there was confrontation with the Labour Council over whether to issue eviction notices.

Meanwhile, Murtagh Diamond claimed that Labour Party had received a flood of new applications for membership, a statement clearly designed to influence the outcome of the Party's selection procedure for choosing their candidates to contest the 1973 local government elections. This would lead to the local Party leadership meeting privately with Regional Labour Party officials to determine how to deal with the matter.[1]

Rebel Jim Davison, in a statement to the Gazette on the 7 October, made clear that he would not return to the Council until the Rent Act had been repealed by a future Labour Government. Davison and his colleague John Wakeford held a public meeting in Biddick Hall in order to explain to tenants why they felt it necessary to resign. They made clear their opposition to the proposed rent strike and urged the 100 tenants in attendance not to break the law.[2]

The former Councillors received criticism from the floor of the meeting — with some residents suggesting that they should have stayed and fought — but both Davison and Wakeford maintained that they had acted as their consciences dictated.

The Progressives were determined to make as much political capital from Labours U-turn as possible. In particular, they protested at the £1 rent rise imposed on Council tenants on the new Woodbine Estate in the centre of the town. In a letter to the Town Clerk, the Secretary of the Progressive Association Edward Russell wrote:

I have been asked by my Executive to express astonishment that houses in the Woodbine and subsequent developments have had their rents increased by the full amount as the present rent is almost up to the 'fair rent'.

I understand that as far back as July 1972, the Borough Treasurer presented a report indicating that even without a rebate these people should only have had a maximum increase of 37p.

I have therefore been asked if you can arrange a special meeting of the Housing Committee to correct this anomaly and ensure that excessive rents are not being charged. [3]

Eddie Russell would endeavour to maintain pressure on the Labour Council on this issue through the letters pages of Shields Gazette.

The October meeting of the Trades Council was dominated by the events of the previous few weeks. In a debate that contained mounting anger at prominent Labour councillors, the meeting discussed a five-point plan devised by Jim Riddle. Riddle told the meeting that their official policy was to resist the Rent Act for as long as they could and his plan sought to achieve this.[4]

Riddle's proposals were:

- A new round of talks with the different tenants associations in the town;
- A renewed leaflet campaign;
- A call to the Chairman of the Housing Committee to reaffirm a pledge that no one will be evicted for refusing to pay a rent increase;
- More active and financial support from all member branches of the Trades Council;
- Combined action with other Trades Councils on Tyneside and Wearside to oppose the Act.

But there was criticism from one Trades Council delegate — and it came from an unlikely source.

Hugh Nicol, a member of AUEW Trade Union and a senior member of the hard-left Socialist Labour League, was hardly noted for his moderate views. In fact he was always a strong advocate of direct militant action in the workplace and his presence is recorded in many editions of the Shields Gazette manning picket lines.

But Nicol opposed a rent strike.

> *It is wrong to tell tenants and housewives that through a rent strike they can bring down the Government. All they can suffer is defeat,*

Nicol told delegates. He continued,

> *Even a united movement could not defeat the Industrial Relations Act.*

Nicol wanted the Trades Council, even at this late stage, to call for a 'retreat with dignity'.[5]

But rebel Councillor Malcolm Campbell maintained his defiance.

> *Rather than retreat with dignity we should strive to win with vigour,*

he said to applause from delegates.

Whilst it was the Trades Councils policy to oppose the Rent Act, said Campbell, it was entirely up to individual tenants associations whether they went on a rent strike, and if they did, the Trades Council would not desert them. Campbell also made clear for the record that if there were to be any evictions, he would be one of the first, because he was withholding the rent increase.[6]

Despite Nicol's objections, the meeting agreed Jim Riddle's five-point plan for action.

Meanwhile, both the Progressive Association and the Labour Party were required to choose candidates for the Biddick Hall by-election which was scheduled to take place on November 23 — just three days after the rents would be formally increased!

At a meeting of Biddick Hall Labour Party members held on the 2 November and with Malcolm Campbell in attendance from the Constituency Executive Committee as an observer, members chose AUEW Union Official Paddy McKay a marine fitter at Middle Docks, and, surprisingly, the retiring Councillor Jim Davison as their candidates.

Latter-day commentators maintain today that Davison chose to re-enter the Council because he was part of an attempt by the hierarchy within the South Shields Labour Party to force the resignation from the Council of Malcolm Campbell. They felt that they could claim that Campbell was being a hypocrite by remaining on the Authority when other opponents of the non-implementation strategy had resigned. Senior Party Officials had long suspected Campbell of being a dangerous influence on the Constituency Party and were determined to close ranks to force him out of local politics (which eventually happened on 6 December).[7]

However, the selection process caused a row within Labour ranks. In particular, Campbell claimed that Party rules had been broken, since Davison was not on the Party's approved list of potential candidates and that the candidates had been chosen by members of the Labour Party's joint 'West Wards Committee', which covered several electoral wards and not just Biddick Hall Labour Party members. Campbell also claimed that new Labour Party members had been prevented from voting. Campbell fired off an angry letter to the Party's National Executive Committee. However the selection meeting had been arranged two days before the final 'Close of nominations' for the election at the Town Hall. The South Shields Labour Party would not meet until after the official deadline and accordingly Campbell still feels today that the whole event was a 'fiddle' by the Labour hierarchy. [8]

But in an emotional Shields Gazette article on the 7 November entitled 'Election candidate hits back at 'rule broken' allegation' (and neatly timed to co-incide with that evening's Labour Management Committee, meeting), Paddy McKay refuted any suggestions that the selection in Biddick Hall had been conducted improperly.

'Councillor Campbell is impugning my character. I am not a dishonest person', said McKay. He continued, 'I am a man of impeccable character,

not a political animal. I have entered the political field to try and do a job honestly and sincerely for the people of Biddick Hall.' [9]

There was, as could be expected, a high turnout at the Labour Management Committee meeting on 7 November. The meeting's Agenda was completely dominated by the events of the previous few weeks. Murtagh Diamond, the Party Chair, said that on the instructions of the Regional Office, he was proposing that the new applicants for membership would not be allowed to take part in the Party's internal selection procedures for the 1973 local government elections. The Party Officers also requested that the Management Committee endorse Davison and McKay for the Biddick Hall by-election.

Again the Party's meeting was bitter and divisive, with Malcolm Campbell being the most vocal in opposition to the selection procedure adopted for Biddick Hall and to the prevention of new

Cllr. Bob Growcott
Photo: Shields Gazette

Party members voting in the selection members. Today, Campbell argues that there was no 'mass infiltration' of Labour's ranks by Tenants Association members; neither had the Trades Council encouraged this.

'If anything...' said Campbell, "...there was drift away from the Labour Party. I think Murtagh Diamond was merely over-acting'. [10]

Bob Growcott, the Party Secretary at the time, agreed with this statement, saying that he had seen a number of torn membership cards posted through the door of the Party headquarters, but no evidence of mass infiltration.

'It could be of course that Murtagh and Liz (Diamond) were concerned that there **may** be an attempt at mass infiltration by the public before the Party selection meetings and accordingly they may have wanted to protect the Party. But certainly, there was no obvious increase in membership'.[11]

On both the issue of Biddick Hall selection and the status of new members, the Party delegates backed Murtagh Diamond and the Party Leadership.

The Labour establishment also defeated a resolution from the

Mineworkers Union calling for the resignation of those Labour Councillors who had supported a 'free vote' and those who had voted to implement the rent Act. The resolution was defeated 40 votes to 14.[12]

Labour Party officers also fired the first shots in their campaign to dislodge Campbell. The minutes of the October Management meeting recorded Campbell advising the meeting that he would resign from the Council if the Rent Act was implemented. Campbell claimed that this was not correct; he had said that he would only resign the Labour Whip. Liz Diamond maintained that the minutes were correct and the meeting agreed them as a true and correct record.

Meanwhile, the Council bureaucracy prepared for the rent increase. On November 17, the Borough Treasurer Sydney Curry announced that many tenants entitled to rent rebates under the Act had still not applied for them. Only 6,750 applications had been received and with the rents due to increase by £1 a week the following Monday he urged people to seek advice. The Council opened an advice centre in Bolingbroke Street in order to assist the tenants as well as placing a number of advertisements in the local press.

The Labour Party faced four opponents at the Biddick Hall by-election. Eddie Russell, the Secretary of the Progressive Association (and a former Horsley Hill Councillor) and George Wilkinson (a former Progressive Councillor in the Bents Ward), together with two 'Independent Socialists' candidates, Mrs Iris Tate and Mr Davison Brennan. Both were active in the Tenants Association but they were not formal candidates from their Association. As a Federation Spokesman explained,

> The Federation is an organisation to promote and protect tenants' interests. It is non-political in the sense that it is above party politics.[13]

John Wakeford acted as the election agent for the Labour Party in the short campaign.

On the eve of the rent increase the South Shields Federation of Tenants Association called a mass meeting to rally the tenants in favour of a rent strike. They distributed over 20,000 leaflets to Council tenants calling upon them to remain steadfast.

The Federation's leaflet proclaimed:

> *When the rent collector calls for the increase, pay your normal rent but refuse to pay the increase.*
>
> *Be polite but firm. Remember the rent collector is only carrying out his orders — he may even be on you side.*
>
> *Don't enter into any argument with him. If he does try to argue with you, call for your neighbour or just close the door.* [14]

Grassby calculated that it would take 12 weeks before rent arrears justified any action against the tenants — during which time they were hoping to persuade the Council not to evict any Council tenants. Other Councils had faced rent strikes following their own decision to implement the Act, but experience had shown that the strikes eventually dwindled through lack of support.[15]

On the eve of the public meeting, Mackley told the rent strike rebel tenants that unless they paid the rent increase they would be evicted. He accused the Trades Council of waging a war against the Labour Council instead of the Conservative Government.

> *It's no good people thinking that the local Trades Council can protect them against their action.* [16]

Mackley was determined to stamp authority on the issue. He claimed that, 'These people are leading tenants up the hill and they certainly won't lead them down again'. In a further show of determination to limit any electoral damage, the Labour Group expelled Malcolm Campbell from membership — this expulsion would ensure that the Constituency Party would be able to prevent his being considered as a possible candidate for the 1973 Council elections.

The public meeting in support of the rent strike saw 200 tenants turn up at the Bolingbroke Hall. The meeting's attention focused upon the

RENT STRIKE

On the 4th October, 1972, the South Shields Labour Council broke its election pledge and voted to implement the Rent Act in South Shields.

Previously 17 Labour Councillors had supported a "free vote" in the Council to allow 11 of their members to vote with the Tories and bring in the Rent Act.

The Labour Council is now collaborating with the Tory Government to operate the Act. You will have been notified of the first £1 increase in your rent to come into effect on the 20th November. Even if you qualify for a rebate **your rent has been increased unnecessarily.**

> **REMEMBER** .... you will lose £1 of your rebate if you look after an aged parent
> .... you will lose £1·50 of your rebate if your child leaves school for work
> .... you will lose 34p for every £2 wage increase or overtime.
>
> **AND REMEMBER** .... your rents will go up another £1 in 1973
> .... and another £1 in 1974
> .... and then the process will start all over again !
>
> **AND ALSO REMEMBER** .... you get NO rebate on rates (see the front of your rent book), and these will shoot up next year due to the Rent Act.

THE ONLY WAY LEFT TO RESIST IS TO REFUSE TO PAY THE RENT INCREASE

Twelve Tenants' Associations have been formed in Shields to support a Rent Strike. Over 1,000 tenants have already said they will NOT pay the rent increase.

If sufficient tenants say they will not pay—NOTHING CAN BE DONE TO FORCE THEM TO PAY.

What YOU can do :

When the rent collector calls for the increased rent—**PAY YOUR NORMAL RENT BUT REFUSE TO PAY THE INCREASE.**

Be polite but firm—remember the rent collector is only carrying out his orders—and he might even be on your side.

Don't enter into an argument with him. If he does try to argue with you, call for your neighbour—or just close the door. Report it later to your Tenants' Association.

What will happen :

Nothing can happen if you refuse to pay the rent increase for at least four weeks. You will have to be the equivalent of at least one full week in arrears before any action is taken—**AND THE CHAIRMAN OF THE HOUSING COMMITTEE HAS SAID HE WILL NOT EVICT ANY TENANTS BECAUSE OF A RENT STRIKE.**

If anyone TRIES to take action against ANY tenant they will be defended by the combined strength of :
> Their Tenants' Association
> The Federation of Tenants' Associations
> The Trades Union Council
> .... and every other tenant on rent strike.

If even ONE tenant is threatened the Trades Union Council will call for industrial strike action by local unions.

Victor Feather and the T.U.C. have pledged their full support. We will demand THEIR help if YOU are threatened.

The Claimants' Union, for those claiming Social Security Benefits, has offered its full support for the strike. They will be available five days a week and ANY tenant on rent strike can call to see them any afternoon Monday to Friday :
> 1.00—3.00 p.m.
> THE PEOPLE'S PLACE (ex-Unitarian Church, Derby Terrace, near public baths).

DON'T WORRY, YOU ARE NOT ALONE, AND YOU WILL NEVER BE LEFT TO FIGHT FOR YOURSELF.

If your rent is paid by Social Security you will NOT be asked to join the rent strike (but you can if you want to help the fight). **But don't pay any increase until you have got it from Social Security.**

What else YOU can do :

SIGN THE PETITION TO THE TOWN COUNCIL—someone will call at your door.

DISPLAY THE POSTERS "SUPPORT THE RENT STRIKE"—available from Tenants' Associations.

ATTEND YOUR NEXT TENANTS' ASSOCIATION MEETING—further details and information about the rent strike will be given there.

ATTEND THE MASSIVE PUBLIC PROTEST DEMONSTRATION TO BE HELD :

SUNDAY 19th NOVEMBER at BOLLINGBROKE HALL
6.00 p.m.

FIGHT BACK .... REFUSE TO PAY THE RENT INCREASE AND **YOU** CAN CHANGE THE LAW .... The Miners did .... The Dockers did .... SO CAN YOU !

SUPPORT THE RENT STRIKE

Council Leader's statement, and tenants demanded assurances from Billy Malcolm that there would be no mass evictions. Albert Elliott said that he had no intention of going back to the Labour Group — 'except to vote against Mackley as Leader'. Malcolm Campbell urged tenants not to believe what was printed in the Gazette because the reports were usually biased against the tenants.[17]

65

The meeting agreed to start the rent strike on Monday 20 November, when the rents were officially increased, and also to approach the Housing Chair and ask him to stand by his word and not allow evictions.

As the rent strike got under way on the Monday morning, Billy Malcolm issued a press statement saying that there would be no mass evictions, but that this did not absolve anyone acting irresponsibly. It was, he said, a case of wait and see.

If there were a considerable number of people going on a rent strike then this is obviously something the Labour group would have to look at, but the final decision would have to be taken by the full Council.

He urged tenants to see if they could receive any subsidies from the Act.

It would be tragic if they went on strike and lost rebates they could quite possibly qualify for. [18]

The by-election in Biddick Hall brought no surprises. Davison and McKay were elected but Labour's majority was down slightly. Given Mackley's public statements about evictions the previous weekend, it was a good result for the Labour Party. The only real excitement in the campaign was someone plastering an election leaflet on Jim Davison's window at home.[19]

Biddick Hall by-election result

Jim Davison (Labour)	568
Paddy McKay (Labour)	567
Eddie Russell (Prog)	170
Davison Brennan (Ind)	166
George Wilkinson (Prog)	157
Iris Tate (Ind)	<u>152</u>
	397 Maj

The turnout was derisory, which considering the nature of the high profile resignations must have been a disappointment to all of the political parties.

The line-up in the Biddick Hall by-election

JIM DAVISON (LAB)   EDDY RUSSELL (PROG)   PADDY McKAY (LAB)   GEORGE WILKINSON (PROG)

Six-way contest fought on rent row

IRIS TATE (IND)

DAVISON BRENEN (IND)

WITH the threat of a mass rents strike hanging over South Shields, Biddick Hall electors go to the polls tomorrow for what has so far proved to be a controversial by-election.

The election is being fought against the stormy background of the Government's Rent Act — the issue that brought resignations from two Labour councillors to create the present vacancies.

It was South Shields council's decision to implement the "fair rents" Act that led to ex-councillors John Wakeford and Jim Davison resigning.

Now Mr Davison is back in the fight in a bid to reclaim his seat.

Six candidates are in the line-up and all are fighting on the rents issue.

Came back

The Progressive line of attack is based on the fact that lower rent increase limits could have won Government approval if sought.

The two Independent Socialists are taking the line of Labour's broken election promise that they would not implement the increase.

But all eyes in this election will be on 42-year-old Mr Davison, the man who resigned and then came back.

Controversy surrounding the by-election was heightened as soon as Mr Davison and the second Labour fighter, Mr Paddy McKay were named as candidates. Coun. Malcolm Campbell (Lab. Rek) objected to the

selection procedure and took his protest to the national executive of the Labour Party in London.

An assistant warehouse and transport manager, Mr Davison won his first council seat in last year's elections.

Third bid

A past student of Ruskin College Oxford, where he studied politics, philosophy and economics, Mr Davison of Carroll Walk, South Shields, is political education officer to the town's Labour Party.

Fighting alongside him is a 43-year-old Mr McKay, a marine fitter at Middle Docks making his third bid for a council seat. He was beaten in Harton Ward in

the last election and West Park the year before.

Mr McKay has been president of South Shields branch of the Amalgamated Union of Engineering Workers for ten years. Married with three children, he lives in Chaucer Avenue.

The two Progressive candidates are Mr George Wilkinson and Mr Eddy Russell, both with council experience behind them.

An accountant

Mr Wilkinson, a 33-year-old electrical fitter at Reyrolle's represented Bents Ward from 1970 until the last election when he was narrowly defeated in a straight fight by Coun. Paddy Cain.

Mr Russell, of Gray's Walk, is 35 and has five years' council experience behind him.

He works as an accountant with a laundry firm at Gateshead. During his council service he was vice-chairman of the Finance Committee as well as serving on the Cultural and Leisure Activities and Libraries Committees.

As well as the main issue of rents, the Progressives will also fight on the sale of council houses which was stopped by the Labour Party after the last election.

In support

Leading the Independent Socialists into the struggle is battling Mrs Iris Tate, the 58-year-old wife of an ex-miner.

Mrs Tate, of Wenlock Place will fight with Mr Davison Brenen in support

Light relief on matter of gravity

A PROGRESSIVE councillor saw the light during discussions at a meeting of South Shields Finance Committee on spending £68,000.

The money was to be spent on building 127 houses and nine garages in Bamburgh Avenue, and discussion had just begun when a light bulb dropped from a chandelier directly above Dr John McKee.

The bulb scored a direct hit on the top of Dr McKee's head, bounced off and shattered as it hit the floor.

Quipped Dr McKee, who was unhurt: "This is the first shot in the by-election," referring to the Biddick Hall poll caused by the resignation of two Labour councillors over the Housing Finance Act.

SPECIAL PURCHASE OF
FIBREGLASS CURTAINING

67

Riddle and other Trades Council activists continued their defiance by holding regular meetings with tenants in order to retain a core group of residents on rent strike. Grassby argues today that over 1,000 tenants were withholding rent although the Council would admit to only 460 at the rent strike's peak. On 26 November, at one of the regular tenants' meetings, allegations were made that rent collectors were using unfair methods in collecting the rent increase, informing tenants refusing to pay the increase that they were the only tenants not to do so. Grassby was outraged — 'their job is to collect the rent that is all. [20]

The elections to the new Tyne and Wear County Council and South Tyneside District would be held in May 1973 and the Party was determined to show a united face to the public. Campbell's expulsion from the Labour Group was merely 'noted' by the December meeting of the South Shields Labour Party Constituency Party. The same meeting was also informed that the new Co-ordinating Committee (an ad hoc Labour committee overseeing the selection of the candidates for the new District elections) had refused to include Albert Elliott, Paddy Cain or Malcolm Campbell in the approved list of possible candidates. Although technically Elliott and Cain were not entitled to be on the candidates list because they had resigned from the Labour Group whilst Campbell was excluded from the Group. In what the Labour Party minutes describe as a 'confused debate' the meeting agreed to recommend support for Albert Elliott and Paddy Cain but not Malcolm Campbell. It was clear that the Party wanted Campbell out.[21]

A day later, on 6 December, Campbell went before he was pushed. He stormed out of the meeting of the Housing Committee after the Committee debated a report on the Rent Strike, claiming that he was serving no purpose there and shouted that he was leaving the Council.

Promises were made by the Labour Party and are not being kept. I am very disappointed at my colleagues, there is no point in being here, when the Act is being carried out by Labour Councillors.[22]

Campbell recalls today that his more vivacious comments were not recorded by the Gazette, '...I also said, in the words of Orwell's book,

Animal Farm, "He looked at the pigs and then the humans, and looked again at the pigs, he could see no difference". And there is no difference here either because you are all Tories'. Campbell remembers receiving a severe reprimand from Billy Malcolm after the meeting for insulting the Labour members.[23]

The Report informed Councillors that out of 16,000 tenants, only 295 had refused to pay the rent increase; the total a week earlier had been 408 and it was clear that the number would drop as the weeks went by. Elliott asked the meeting to agree not to evict any tenant on rent strike, but this found no support and the Committee insisted that anyone on rent strike should be treated the same way as other tenant.

Councillor Jim Hodgson (who voted against implementation and initially resigned from the Group over the issue) said that he had no intention of backing a rent strike, 'People have got to pay the increase whether they like it or not'.[24]

Campbell's departure was 'regretted' by Billy Malcolm, who said that in time he would have become a valuable member of the Council.

People found him a little extreme, I always had a certain regard for him.

However, Malcolm said that he always favoured opposing the Act, but South Shields could not do it alone. Jim Florence said that Campbell was a 'maverick' whilst Liz Diamond was more forthright, describing him as a 'big head'. Yet all observers agreed that Campbell was sincere in his belief and opposition to the Rent Act. He alone, they all agree, was the one man who would have been prepared to go to jail over non-implementation.

The same meeting also received a Report from the Council Officers advising that South Shields Council was £125,000 short in its housing revenue account because of the delay in implementing the Act. The Authority hoped that the new Environment Secretary Geoffrey Rippon would not insist that the default had to be made up. Instead, the Housing Committee decided to apply to him for exemption from the provisions of the Act from October 2 until November 20 — the seven-week period during which the £1 increase was not imposed.[25]

The Housing Committee agreed to advise Rippon that £80,000 in interest on revenue from the sale of council houses would be going into the housing revenue account. They also claimed that their original decision not to implement was based upon the uncertain passage of the Bill through Parliament and the fact that the Council's Committee procedure meant that a final decision could not be made until October 4 and that the preparation and notices would take another four weeks.

However, Stan Smith rejected the explanation for the delay, claiming that the Labour Councillors had been intent on breaking the law.

It is clear that the delay in implementation was a political act and that money from the sale of the Council houses should not be used to bail out some of the Labour Council. [26]

Meanwhile, without the support of Labour Councillors and with a disappointing lack of support from tenants, together with the collapse of the organised rent strike nationally, the Trades Council realised that they had to arrange a dignified retreat on the rent strike. It duly came on 10 December 1972.

The Federation voted 38-11 to end the first phase of the tenants' action. A 'second phase' of militant action would commence, they valiantly claimed, on 1 February 1973 when private tenants found that their rents had been increased and the Council was required to increase the rents further. Jim Florence, a member of the Federation, said that they could not have hoped to succeed when less than one hundred people were part of the strike.

The Labour Party were described as the 'Sweeney Todds' who had let the people down, but as Jim Florence pointed out, the Association and the Trades Council had not received the support of the tenants of South Shields.

Meanwhile, a similar rent strike by Low Simonside residents in Jarrow was also on the verge of collapsing. Residents had requested a meeting with Jarrow Councillors to discuss the consequences of not paying the rent increases but this was flatly rejected.

Councillor Brian Howard told the Jarrow Council's Housing Committee that most of the town's Council tenants were paying their rent and that such a meeting would set a 'dangerous precedent'.[27]

Malcolm Campbell, who had still to officially resign from the Council, urged the South Shields tenants to stick together and make the Associations work:

> ...there are many more struggles coming not just under the Housing Act and to prove this to be a tactical retreat is to stay together.

Grassby told the meeting that the fight could have been won if the Labour Party had backed them.

> We have seen this rent strike against a background of a Labour Council which has changed from being against the Act to supporting it. The Council has predicted that this Federation will not last until Christmas. It is up to this meeting to show that this is not true. [28]

Echoing Hugh Nicol's earlier sentiments, he described the ending of the Rent Strike as a 'dignified retreat'.

However, many tenants active in the local Associations felt that they had taken part on a march with the Grand old Duke of York. The Associations began to crumble and one individual narrowly escaped arrest for attacking a rent collector in the Cleadon Park area of town. Although Mike Peel recalls that the Trades Council should have been more suspicious of him when, for a third time, they heard him recite his 'Magna Carta' speech (word for word each time he made it) on the rights of the ordinary citizens. [29]

All the leading advocates for a rent strike maintain today that over 1,000 tenants had taken part. Campbell believes that the Council Officers and the Gazette newspaper were manipulating the figures. Grassby says today that the intelligence the Rent Strike leaders were receiving was that the strike was strong initially but without the support of the Labour Party it could not be maintained.

Mike Peel observes today:

rearguard rent action

...thinking about it now, it is clear that the frenetic activity of the Trades Council to promote and sustain a rent strike on a borough-wide scale was mildly utopian, tactically inappropriate and destined to fail. The rent strike was unsustainable because other neighbouring authorities had decided to implement the rent increases... [30]

nemployment in the north
:kets towards 100,000, the
:est of the Tory Rent Act
1 a concrete way the road
1930s.

rights of the working
:s standard of living and
unions can only be
:d today in the complete
ation of the working class
ieneral Strike to remove
y government from office.
All Trades Unions Alli-
:mand for the building of
:cil of Action in South
must be taken up as the
:ans of halting the craven
of Labour councils before
:ries' offensive.

also means bringing
r tenants' associations,
nionists, unemployed and

Mike Peel, assistant secretary South Shields Trades Council

Malcolm Campbell recalls,

Perhaps I was naïve but I merely followed Party policy by voting not to implement the Rent Act. I was the one described as a 'traitor' to the Party when the whole episode had blown over. I did not have any real ambitions to be a working-class hero although I would have gone to jail. I just felt that Rent Act was wrong and had to be opposed.

For Campbell the whole affair was to prove a sobering experience. He continued to refuse to pay the rent increase and today maintains that the episode was a contributory factor in the break-up of his marriage.

My wife had reservations about the rent strike. She was a Catholic and I've no doubt under pressure from the Diamonds who were also Catholics. Eventually we split. I left money for her because I would not see her suffer, but I informed the Housing Department that I personally would not pay the increase and today I am still proud to say I didn't.

Campbell left the town and went to sea, becoming active in the Seaman's Union where he supported left-wing Jim Slater's bid to become General Secretary of the Union — *'Although that didn't stop him on three occasions trying to expel me from the Union!'* [31]

Chapter 5

The Revolution delayed

The old fight has gone
Brian Lister, letter to
Shields Gazette, 11th October 1972

The beginning of 1973 saw that emergence of new concerns for the Labour and Trade Union movement in South Shields.

Industrial disputes occurred along the river Tyne; the powerful local Mineworkers Union was embroiled in legal action with one of its members over a local Lodge Rule, and the whole trade union movement was in confrontation with the Tory Government over the Industrial Relations Act.

Meanwhile, elections to the new South Tyneside Metropolitan Borough Council (which brought together the County Borough of South Shields and the smaller councils of Jarrow, Hebburn and Boldon) and the new Tyne and Wear County Council would take place in April and May 1973. Labour activists were busy selecting their candidates to contest the seats, whilst senior politicians in the Town Hall were locked in battle as to what to call the new local Authority.

Despite the public statements and the disagreements over exactly how many Council tenants were on a rent strike, Grassby and his colleagues knew that the fight was over — there would be no 'phase 2', despite earlier announcements.

The local Labour Party ruthlessly closed ranks, whilst the Shields Gazette refused to accept Trades Council adverts which advertised their regular meetings. The rebels' only 'true believer', Malcolm Campbell, tendered his resignation from the Council immediately following the New Year holiday on 3 January 1973.

Another Shields councillor quits over rent Act

A SOUTH SHIELDS councillor walked out of a housing meeting — and announced his resignation from the town council over the "fair rents" Act. Coun. Malcolm Campbell (Rekendyke), condemning Labour colleagues for their attitude to a tenants' rent strike, said: "I am serving no purpose here."

He told members of the Housing Committee: "Promises were made by the Labour Party, and are not being kept. I am very disappointed with my colleagues. There is no point in being here when the Act is being carried out by Labour councillors."

Coun. Campbell said he was the only councillor advocating a rent strike as the way to fight the Housing Finance Act. After his walkout, the committee was told that at the end of last week 295 out of more than 16,000 tenants had refused to pay the £1 increase, 2.4 per cent of all tenants. The total a week earlier had been 408.

The committee decided that tenants who did not pay the increase should be treated in the same way as others in arrears.

A proposal by Coun. Albert Elliott (Lab., Brinkburn), that none of the tenants on rent strike should be evicted, found no supporters. Coun. Elliott revealed that he was withholding the increase as a protest.

Chairman, Coun. William Malcolm (Lab., Rekendyke), said that there would be no mass evictions. But the council could not "underwrite" individuals who were in arrears.

'Very sincere'

"We cannot meet tenants to discuss the question of evictions. The decision on that is ours and ours alone. But we are very reluctant in South Shields to evict anyone, because of the hardship it causes and the problems it gives to social service departments," said Coun. Malcolm.

He said he was sorry Coun. Campbell had decided to resign. "He was a very sincere councillor, although some people thought he was a little extreme. I have always had a certain regard for him, and in time he would have been a valuable member."

Coun. Malcolm said the Labour Party had opposed the Act, but when the majority of local authorities decided to implement it, South Shields could not stand alone in defiance.

Came back

Coun. Douglas Ridley (Lab., Simonside) said the tenants on rent strike had been badly advised and badly led. "I appeal to them to use a bit of sense."

Coun. James Hodgson (Lab., Cleadon Park) said the council had been "held over a barrel" by the Tory Government. He did not support the Act, but had no intention of backing a rent strike. "People have got to pay the increase whether they like it or not."

Coun. Campbell, member for Rekendyke, is the third Labour councillor to resign over the Act. One of them, Jim Davison, changed his mind and is back on the council, but Mr John Wakeford stuck to his decision.

COUN. CAMPBELL

Cheerful job is a-begging

SANTA may not be coming to Jarrow this year — because he is shy.

Several traders in the town's shopping centre decided it would be a good idea to employ a Santa. He would walk around the shops chatting to youngsters.

However, Mr Paul Perry, one of the traders, has asked 35 elderly people to take on the job — without success. "They all seem to be too shy," he said.

The traders are prepared to pay a man £2 for three hours' work every Thursday, Friday and Saturday until Christmas.

Meanwhile, Mr Perry is trudging the streets looking for a volunteer. Inside a case he is carrying is a complete red-and-white Santa outfit, with beard.

FESTIVE

Blackb Jarrow in fron

A BLACKBERRYING five-year-old boy, a S The boy was chasing ran in front of a car Jarrow. John Paul W Jarrow, died almo coroner Mr Montagu returned a verdict of

Mr Gerald Whipp, o who was in a car drivin saw the boy run down the coming the other way him. He ran from the ver

Mrs Irene Cooper, of R the car in the accident, she was driving at 40 t mph when she came to railway bridge by the Bo Colliery slip road.

The boy came out behind a bridge support, continued running on to road, looking straight a She braked and swerved could not avoid hitting h

Mr Frederick Stobbar Cooper Street, Roker, a enger in the car, said h not see the boy until he

Shields Gazette Jan 7 1972

Writing to the Town Clerk, he said:

It has become obvious to me that the power structure of the Party political system on the Town Council allows a small clique to dictate policy contrary

to the expressed views of the electors of the town. Indeed it has become clear that the political structure has been designed and maintained with this intention.[1]

Even in resigning, Campbell caused controversy.

The County Borough of South Shields would cease to exist in May 1974 and the intermediate arrangements for local government meant that there was no requirement to fill the Rekendyke vacancy.

Progressive George Wilkinson — who had been defeated in the Biddick Hall by-election just a few months earlier — wrote to the Gazette decrying Campbell's resignation as preventing the electors of Rekendyke from having full representation in the Town Hall. Wilkinson maintained that Campbell should have resigned before January 1973, which would have necessitated a by-election. The letter ends with a tongue-in-cheek assertion that if a contest had been held, on the basis of the result in Biddick Hall a few months earlier, Labour would have lost the seat.[2]

This claim was quickly disputed by John Wakeford, who advised Wilkinson that the Progressives had polled 38.8% less in the by-election than their previous figure in May 1965 — hardly a swing to the Progressives.[3]

Jim Riddle said that he felt at the time that he was helping to build a new Jerusalem.

I was gutted when the strike ended — I felt so sure we could have won.[4]

The Progressives maintained their own pressures on the Labour Party within the Council Chamber.

Stan Smith was determined that the ruling Labour Group should be reported to the District Auditor for failing to implement the Act earlier. The decision to implement the Act was made on October 4 but the rents were not increased until November 20, which resulted in lost revenue of £125,000.

The Council had written to the District Auditor requesting an exemption from the payment of the £125,000.

The Authority gave four reasons for their delay in implementing the Rent Act:

- The delay in the Bill becoming an Act;
- The time taken by Committee and Council procedure;
- Administrative time taken to put the Act into operation;
- The need to give four clear weeks notice of a rent increase to their tenants.
- The rebellious decisions taken at a number of Council meetings earlier were not recorded.

At the January full Council meeting on the 3 January, opposition Leader Stan Smith said that the Council house tenants had been badly misled and badly advised about rent strikes and possible eviction. He laid the blame firmly at the feet of Jack Grassby, Billy Malcolm, Ernie Mackley and Vincent Fitzpatrick (the Authority's Mayor).

Smith alleged that the Council had failed to give the full facts to the District Auditors for the £125,000 deficit in revenue on the rent account and listed the decisions taken by his Labour counterparts at various Housing and Management Board meetings in which they had failed to implement the Rent Act.

He ridiculed Labour's Paddy Cain as saying that if Labour won the May 1972 elections they would not implement the Act.

If Councillor Cain had been a man like Councillor Campbell he would have stuck to his guns and would have resigned over the Act.

Smith moved that the minutes of Council meeting recording the decisions on the Act should be sent to the District Auditor.

In response, Billy Malcolm said that it was a bad law that had to be surrounded by penalty clauses to make it work. Councils refusing to implement the Act were faced with the mounting debts and the money would have had to come from ratepayers and council tenants. Labour had, Malcolm maintained, opposed the Act before it was implemented hoping that the Bill would be withdrawn in Parliament. Once it was the law of the land, they had to decide whether the town would be saddled with growing debts.

In a named vote within the Council Chamber, Smith's motion was defeated.[5]

But this did not deter the Progressives; they sent their own dossier to the Auditor. The dossier pointed out that the decision not to implement the Act was made by the Labour Party before the May 1972 local elections and that "The elections were fought, and won, by the Labour Party on this issue".[6]

Meanwhile, with elections to the proposed new South Tyneside Council in just four months, a spirit of unity broke out within Labour's ranks. At their Annual Meeting on the 6 February Jim Davison soundly defeated a Mr Khan for the Chairmanship of the Constituency party whilst Vincent Fitzpatrick became the new Vice-chair.

The minutes recall that in his Agent's report, Jim Doneghan referred to the resignations of Wakeford and Davison (but not Campbell) and called for peace in the party in view of the elections taking place in May for the new South Tyneside Council.

> *We don't want any splits in the party as we have had in the past with one half going one way and the rest going the other.*

Doneghan's comments followed those of Mackley, who advised the Annual meeting that the party had emerged from a very difficult period.

> *The Act caused considerable discord within the Group and Party, culminating in some members resigning. But the Group has survived and is now actively engaged in preparing for the new District elections.*[7]

Surprisingly, at this time, both the Labour Party and Trades Council allowed members of the press to attend Constituency meetings to report on proceedings. In further testament that the times were changing, the March meeting of the Labour Party Management Committee voted to end the practice.

There was only one ray of sunshine for the South Shields Federation of

Tenants Associations and that was the decision of the Town Hall Union NALGO to request advice from their head office on how to maintain defiance of the Act.

A spokesman for the Union said that one of the ways open was for tenants to make an immediate appeal against the assessment of their 'fair rents'. The aim was to block the system with so many appeals as to make the system unworkable.[8]

However, this course of action — although supported by the Federation — seems not to have been taken seriously by the tenants. Tenants were more concerned about ensuring their repairs were undertaken by the Authority, and one of the more active Associations, in Cleadon Park, sent a list of complaints from over 200 residents to the Town Hall, "I am expecting more", said Bernard Appleton, Chair of the Association. However, even this had political undercurrents, Appleton just eight weeks later was selected as the Labour Party's official candidate for Cleadon Park by 18 votes to 17.[9]

But this appears to have been the only sign of positive action by a Tenants Association following the ending of the rent strike. Without the impetus of a 'single issue' to spur them on and keep the tenants together, the Associations quickly collapsed.

Grassby stood down as Secretary of the Trades Council when their Annual meeting was held on the 20 February.

He had led the Trades Council since its 'split' with Labour Party three years earlier. The Trades Council under his leadership was the most militant and pugnacious in the region and he delivered a new left-wing campaign style never experienced in the town before.

Jim Riddle defeated Hugh Nicol for the Secretaryship by 34 votes to 9. Malcolm Campbell endeavoured to carve a niche for himself by defeating Councillor Vi Webster (who had rebelled and voted for implementation of the rent Act) for the Presidency of the Trades Union Council by an equally large margin of 38 votes to 6. However, without Grassby's drive and intellect, the South Shields Trades Council ceased to have the influence that it had in his heyday.[10]

In his Annual Report to members, a bitterly disappointed Grassby accused local Labour leaders of lacking in courage or honesty over the 'Fair rents' Act.

Grassby said that 1972 had been a year in which relations with the local Labour Party went through a 'critical stage':

> *The predictable reasons were because we were celebrating our separate, independent, non-party political role and insisted on our right to pursue our own policies in our own way.*

> *While we could have expected some pulling of the apron strings we could also have hoped for some understanding, if not support from the Labour Party and the Labour Council.*

Instead of having had support, Grassby maintained, the Trades Council was attacked and feared by the Labour Party because the Trades Council was perceived to constitute a threat to the power structure of the Labour establishment.

Jim Riddle   *Photo: Shields Gazette*

Nothing could better demonstrate this than in the fair rents issue. In May, Grassby wrote, the Councillors set out as 'socialist heroes' with a policy of non-implementation. By October when the Council decided to implement the Act, the Labour leaders were reduced to ordinary frightened little men and women, scared by the consequences of their socialist audacity.

We cannot blame them for being ordinary, but we can regret that they had neither the courage to sustain their self-assumed heroic role, nor the political honesty to put the decision to the democratic test of the tenants' vote.

But the Trades Council policy had its price. Grassby advised the Annual Meeting that the local Journalists Union had disaffiliated from the Trades Council and they had failed to attract some white-collar unions into their fold.[11]

Today Grassby remains philosophical. In his book, ***The Unfinished Revolution***, he writes;

As an issue, the Rent Strike failed, yet in South Shields alone some thousand tenants were engaged in direct political action. Certainly it was a defining moment for the relationships between the South Shields Trades Union Council and the Labour Group and Constituency Labour Party — and a watershed for many individual members of the Labour Movement. [12]

For Mike Peel, as a young miner and Trades Council activist, the 1970s proved to be heady and from a radical socialist point of view, optimistic.

Political battles and industrial disputes were being won. The more cautious comrades, especially those who served as Councillors, were disdained because of their caution...those bitten by the fervour of the times were neither evil nor dense (neither were the 'opponents' who sought implementation). Some of the Trades Council activists did show some of the zeal of converts to a messianic faith but the portents of radical change were at the time very real. [13]

For Growcott, the whole episode shattered his idealism as a young councillor.

I idolised Billy Malcolm. The younger Councillors like Dougie Ridley, Dickie Barry, Jim Hodgson and John Dent all did. He was in effect our leader. We would spend hours at his barber shop talking politics, I'm sure he must have lost hundreds of pounds as customers came in, took one look at the crowd and left.

But after the vote to implement, long-standing friendships were never the same. Maybe in hindsight we should have resigned from the Council and then again looking back now, perhaps Billy was right. He must have thought long and hard about the consequences to his family and the Party when he was in Scarborough. There was certainly not the backlash we feared from the electorate, we may even have been left high and dry by them if we had broken the Law.[14]

K. Sklair, writing for the **Socialist Register** in 1975, has pointed out that there were three groups of Labour authorities which chose not to comply with the Housing Finance Act in the months immediately following its passage:

1: Those who never implemented the rent rise, Clay Cross and the Welsh authority of Bedwas and Machen (but Bedwas permitted the Housing Commissioner to raise the rents)

2: Those who held out into 1973 (Conisborough, Biggleswade and Camden in England, Merthyr in Wales and Clydebank, Cumbernauld, Denny, Saltcoats, Whitburn, Alloa, Barrhead, Midlothian and Cowdenbeath in Scotland)

3: 32 Councils implementing after October 1972 but before January 1973 (South Shields included) [15]

Thus, resistance to the Rent Act was left to the small Urban District Council in Derbyshire, Clay Cross. One of its leading members, David Skinner (brother of firebrand MP, Dennis), visited South Shields at the invitation of the Young Socialists, whilst the April Management Committee of the Constituency Party held a special collection for the Clay Cross fighting fund and raised £4.

The eleven rebellious Clay Cross councillors were eventually disqualified from Office and surcharged £6,985 in January 1974 for

81

their defiance. They looked to the new Labour Government elected in the February of the same year for support — they would be disappointed. The Prime Minister, Harold Wilson, told the House of Commons on 4 April that there would be no contribution from the public funds to ease the financial burden on the former councillors, The law of the land, however unfair, however oppressive, must be obeyed until it is repealed.[16]

However, whilst refusing to examine the question of the surcharge, the new Labour Government did intend in its new Housing Finance (Special Provisions) Legislation to make provision for the recovery of debts incurred under the Rent Act but without the debt falling directly as a personal charge against the councillors. The loss would be collected from ratepayers and tenants.

Wilson shifted part of the responsibility for the Clay Cross rebellion on to local residents but failed to relieve the Council rebels of their own personal responsibility for defying the legislation.

Clay Cross UDC was eventually merged into the new North East Derbyshire District Council (NEDDC) in May 1974. Meanwhile, the £87,959 shortfall in 'lost' rents uncovered by the District Auditor had to be recovered by the residents of Clay Cross.

> *With such an imposition being placed on the former UDC residents, with NEDDC's Labour Group disowning the rebels and with the militant councillors bankrupted and removed from office, it was rather ironical that the Ratepayers Association was able to capitalise upon Labour's plight by taking all six Clay Cross seats on NEDDC and entering a Conservative/Independent/Ratepayer coalition.* [17]

In April 1973, the electors of South Shields went to the polls to elect their representatives to the new Tyne and Wear County Council. The polls held no shocks for Labour with Ernie Mackley, Billy Malcolm and his brother Harry being three of Labour's victors. George Smith was also elected, becoming the first Conservative member to win an election in South Shields under the Conservative banner.

The electors went back to the polls in May 1973 to elect their representatives to the new South Tyneside District Council. Mackley

S Shields Gazette, Thursday, March 28, 1974

Stormy scene as sides clash over fair rents

TOWN COUNCIL

COUN. MADSEN   ALD RICHARDSON

NO CHANGE OF LAND DECISION

THE chairman of the Town Improvement Committee defended its members' action in refusing to sell land, on lease from the council to a supermarket chain.

Amos Hinton and Co. Ltd. had been negotiating with the council over the purchase of the freehold interest of the land in Queen Street where they have already been given permission to build a supermarket.

Coun. Alan Madsen (Prog. Beacon) asked the council if it was not possible to reverse the decision of the committee and sell the land for a supermarket chain.

THE HANDLING of "fair rents" in South Shields in 1972 — which left £5,610 to come out of the general rate fund — caused a stormy scene at the last meeting of South Shields Town Council.

The council was moving the report of the District Auditor in which it was stated that the seven-week delay caused by the then all-Labour Management Board's decision not to implement the Housing Finance Act had resulted in £100,000 not collected in rents, with more than £5,000 of this to come out of the general rate fund.

The reversal of this decision by the council nearly two months later, said it had been done so that the Management Board could be taken to task and possibly deferred from office for five years and forced to pay surcharges.

"We were being asked to implement something that was not legal" he said. "The Progressive Council could have started the policy much earlier, but they refused to do so. This really is the thin edge of the wedge as far as democracy is concerned."

Coun. Malcolm was speaking after Ald. Harry Marshall (Prog.) expressed his own disappointment at the way the matter had been handled.

"Something could have been done by the Council it they wanted to" he said "but they didn't. They could have called a special meeting and you would have been given the right to express an opinion contrary to our own."

The £30,000 to £35,000 which had been offered for it — Progressive Council would have started the policy much earlier, but they refused to be invested.

But the action of the committee was defended by its chairman, Ald. Jack Richardson (Lab.).

"The town, I think, should retain as much control as it can in its central development area" he said.

"You talk about the amount of money which has been offered for it — the possibility of its being invested. But this wouldn't be the case It would be swallowed up in the general activities of the council which succeeds us."

ALL-IN SCHOOLS DISSENT AMONG THE TRIBUTES

DISSENT crept into the meeting during a speech on comprehensive education by Coun. Mrs Elizabeth Diamond (Lab., Brinkburn), chairman of South Shields Education Committee.

After she had told the council: "I have done my duty as an educationist and Socialist," Ald. Mrs Margaret Sutton (Lab.) retorted that all the spadework for comprehensive education had been done before Coun. Mrs Diamond came into the matter.

It had been on the cards since 1968, said Ald. Mrs Sutton, herself a former education chairman, but it had never been possible to get through the council. There had also been opposition from the town's teachers who saw comprehensive schools as

COUN. MALCOLM

History chapter closed on sad evening

MORE than 120 years of history came to an end with the last meeting of South Shields Town Council.

Looking fit and well after his short spell in hospital, the Mayor, Coun. Ken Scrimger, signed the council minutes for the last time and accepted the past Mayor and Mayoress' badges.

The Mayor and Mayoress, Coun. Mrs Elizabeth Scrimger, had seen through an arduous year, said Ald. Ernest Mackley (Lab.) in the vote of thanks.

"They have, in addition, to the bigger responsibilities of being Mayor and Mayoress, both been extremely ably carried out their many social duties with dignity. They have been a credit to the town and to the party."

DONE DUTY

Thanking the deputy Mayor and Mayoress, coun. Murtagh and Elizabeth Diamond, Coun. William Malcolm (Lab. Rekendyke) said it had been a good year because it had been one that had seen the council slowly dying.

"But you have done your duty," he said, "with dignity and your example has reminded us all of our great history and tradition. I am sure you will be remembered with affection by everyone who has had the pleasure of ...

The last round-up

THOSE who attended the final meeting of South Shields Town Council were Aldermen J Abbot, M Abey, I Caplan, R Dodds, J R Donkin, E Hill, E Mackley, G Maguire, H Marshall, W ...

---

headed the poll in Simonside, whilst Billy Malcolm did the same in Rekendyke. This was despite Progressive leaflets requesting electors to remember that:

> *Council rents were increased despite a solemn promise to tenants.*[18]

It was not until March 1974, at the final meeting of the South Shields County Borough Council, that the Authority was given the decision by the District Auditor in relation to its refusal to raise the rents.

In a stormy debate, the Council was informed that the seven-week delay caused by the all-Labour Management Board's refusal not to implement the Rent Act had resulted in £100,000 not being collected in rent, of which more than £5,610 would need to come from the Council's General Rate Fund. The burden of the balance fell upon the Council tenants.

Billy Malcolm, speaking about the reversal of this decision by the Council two months later, told Council colleagues that it had been done so that the Management Board could be taken to task by the District

Auditor and possibly debarred from office for five years and forced to pay surcharges.

We were being asked to implement something that was not legal.

Malcolm taunted the Progressives that they could have implemented the Bill before it became Law when they held power prior to the 1972 elections, but they had refused. This really is the thin edge of the wedge as far as democracy is concerned, he said.

Progressive Alderman Harry Marshall, expressed regret at the way in which they whole episode had been handled. He told the Chamber:

Something could have been done by the Council if they wanted to, but they didn't. They could have called a special meeting and you would have been given the right to express an opinion contrary to your own [the other council members]. [19]

It had been 17 months since the Town Council had voted to implement the Housing Finance Act. The tenants may have forgiven the Labour Party for its change of heart — the opposition clearly had not.

Afterword

A little rebellion now and then is a good thing.
Thomas Jefferson

At the February 1973 meeting of the Labour Party's Management Committee, under the 'Labour Group Report', Ernie Mackley advised members 'not a lot was happening of note'. [1]

In less than a year he had led his Group from the opposition benches and through a gruelling election campaign that saw him seize the Council leadership. His Party refused to implement the Rent Bill if it became Law but he later advised his colleagues to allow the Council Officers to implement the rent increases. This resulted in a no confidence motion in his leadership — which he won. After this he supported a free vote for the Labour members in the Council Chamber, thus effectively implementing the Rent Act in South Shields. Following this he advised those on a rent strike that they would be evicted and appealed for unity as Councillors resigned the Labour Whip.

Quite a lot **had** been happening.

For Grassby, the lessons from the rent strike were to be applied directly to the fight against the Poll Tax in the late 1980s.

> *This time the action was to prove more successful. Tenants had learned of the impotence of the main political parties and the necessity to construct their own grassroots organisations. Councillors had learned of the dangers of bravado rhetoric.* [2]

In the same tone, Mike Peel felt that valued lessons were learned,

> *The internecine conflict spawned in part by the Housing Finance Act should supply a caution about how those of us who opposed the Poll Tax should mount our opposition to it.* [3]

It is perhaps ironical that 18 years after the implementation of the Rent

Act, the author, son of the previous Housing Chairman, Billy Malcolm, would be the Chairman of South Tyneside Council's Finance Committee charged with the implementation of the Poll Tax in the Borough.

Even more ironic is that the Leader of the Council during the Poll Tax period would be Albert Elliott, who resigned the Labour Whip in October 1972 following the decision to implement the Act in the Town.

Lessons were certainly learned.

No promises in the Labour Party election literature — except a vague call to the electorate to 'oppose the Poll Tax'; no motions demanding non-implementation at Labour Party meetings; no mass meetings; no action groups, and certainly no demonstrations.

Those who chose the extreme route of direct action were fringe political activists and they did not even belong to the local Trades Council, whose organisational strength was depleted by mass unemployment and a dearth of new young trade union blood within its ranks.

South Tyneside was one of the first Authorities to implement the Poll Tax and as a result South Tyneside Magistrates were the first to send someone to prison for non-payment of the Tax.

Could it all have been so different in 1972?

By May 1972 the local Labour Party had been out of power for three years. Within a further two, the County Borough of South Shields would cease to exist and it would bring within its borders Jarrow, Hebburn and Boldon into a new District Authority.

Before that occurred, senior Councillors from each of the four Authorities would meet regularly to plan the transition. Jarrow, Hebburn and Boldon would, without question, be sending Labour representatives to that new Liaison Committee.

Mackley was determined that South Shields — as the biggest town and the administrative centre for the new Authority — would be represented by Labour politicians. But first, he had to win the May 1972 Council elections.

Whether there was a specific promise NOT to implement the Rent Act in the Party's literature and through public statements (and I believe there was) was of no real consequence to the overall election results in May 1972. There had been a drift back to the Labour Party over the previous two elections and Labour's victory in '72 was probably inevitable.

There was no great debate in the letters page of the Shields Gazette (unlike the 1975 Council elections over the issue of Councillors' attendance allowances). Surviving candidates from that era also testify that the issue of the Rent Bill going through Parliament at the time was not of paramount importance to the electorate.

Had there been no such pledge from Mackley in April 1972, Labour would, in all probability, still have decisively won the May elections.

But the Rent Bill **was** an issue of great importance to political activists both on the Right and Left of British politics. To the Left, its main aim was to reduce and eventually eliminate all subsidies to Council housing. To the Right, subsidies would in future go to those in need and would not be a flat rate blanket subsidy — and that did not just mean those in Council rented accommodation.

South Shields was certainly not the only Constituency Labour Party to express outright opposition. In the City of Newcastle the entire Labour Group voted against its implementation (although they had the luxury of being in opposition at the time). Wallsend, Felling, Carlisle and Gateshead were all authorities pledged never to implement the rent increase.

Even within national Labour Party circles, there was a clear belief that if they stood firm, the Bill could be defeated. A special edition of the 'Labour Weekly', produced by the Labour Party headquarters in London at the time, advised that the Housing Finance Act would result in a major battle with Heath Government.

The newspaper claimed:

> *The Government has given itself vast powers to crush any resistance. Tenants can be fined £50 for 'obstructing' a 'fair rent' officer from coming in to inspect. Councillors can be fined £400 for refusing to give information. Labour Councils are totally opposed to the crazy idea of making a profit out of Council tenants.* [4]

Added to this, we have the local Trades Council at the height of its influence, demonstrated by its involvement in the Claimants Union, the Pensioners Movement and individual Trade Unions. The Trades Council worked assiduously with the tenants, determined to create a bedrock of support against implementation of the Act.

This was the environment in which Mackley felt safe to issue the 'non-implementation' call in April 1972 to the South Shields electorate.

But the new Council Leadership had been under a misapprehension that all they needed to do was refuse to implement the Act and a Government Commissioner would instruct the Council Officials on their behalf. This Pontius Pilate approach would ensure the Law was upheld without the Council leadership's losing face.

The Environment Secretary's letter to the Authority (Appendix 2) laid those plans to rest when he made clear the Commissioner would not issue such an instruction until the Council was in default and running up debts. This would ultimately have meant surcharges and disqualification from office for the Council members.

That is when the realism set in.

The Council Leadership, within days, convened a Labour Group meeting and allowed officials to begin preparations for the rent increase; within a month the crucial free vote was given in the Labour Group, which paved the way for the necessary vote in the Council Chamber. Observers today still maintain that some Labour Councillors were openly counting on their figures making sure that enough of their colleagues had voted for the implementation of the Act, before announcing their own heroic opposition to its implementation.

These were the reluctant rebels.

Writing in the Shields Gazette, a Mr. Brian Lister wrote:

> *Nor can I see them (the electors), being too keen on the fence sitters who voted in favour of refusing to implement the Act knowing fine well that there were enough of their colleagues prepared to commit political hara kari to get it introduced. I am sure that may of them deep down did not want to oppose the Act's implementation, but they were too afraid of their political future to stand up and be counted.* [5]

Without realising it at the time — the Labour activists in South Shields were in many respects playing out a battle which would be carried out with greater ferocity in the movement in the 1980s: the battle for the soul of the Labour Party.

On the one hand was the left-wing Trades Council who advocated the policies of direct action and the active involvement of local communities in the issues which affected their everyday lives. They believed that they had an unalienable right to defy an unjust law. On the other hand there was moderate municipal Labourism that had a stanglehold on civic affairs.

What changed in the 1980s in places like the GLC, Lambeth, Liverpool and Islington, is that the tactics of direct action advocated by the left had replaced municipal Labourism as the dominant force in many Town Halls. Not since 1921, when George Lansbury and his fellow Poplar Councillors refused to set a rate, had such defiance of the Law by elected members come to the fore.

And on every occasion — (even if they achieved some minor victories at the time) whether it be Hatton's Liverpool, Livingstone's London, Skinner's Clay Cross or Lansbury's Poplar — the centre ensured their ultimate defeat. A similar fate would have awaited Mackley's South Shields.

Which brings us to the whole question of the rule of the law and its defiance by elected representatives.

For Malcolm Campbell, the issue was clear, he was elected on a mandate to oppose the Housing Finance Act and was acting in line with the official policy of the South Shields Labour Party. He believes he had a right to disobey the law as the only effective means of opposing the Act.

Many activists in the Trades Council would argue that they were right to disobey an unjust law that to them was 'political' in that it discriminated against Council tenants.

The opposite view for Labour moderates like Liz Diamond and Jim Doneghan were just as clear. Democracy depends upon the rule of law. We cannot pick and choose between laws we like and dislike and it follows that we must obey all laws until they are changed. As Dick Taverne, the former Independent Labour MP for Lincoln, points out, this view has a respectable ancestry. Its most extreme exponent was Socrates, who refused to escape when he was condemned to death, even though he had been wrongly condemned under an unjust law in a dictatorial state. He duly drank the hemlock, as the law required.[6]

Again, a mandate from the voters is no excuse. A mandate to oppose a law is not a mandate to break it — even if the electorate supports a specific pledge to break a particular law. Indeed, every elected member is pledged to obey the law as a condition of holding public office.

And whatever twists, plots, whispers or U-turns occurred at the time — it is this argument that eventually won through in South Shields Town Hall 30 years ago.

Appendix 1

Bibliography and references

Chapter 1 – A Fair Deal for Housing

1:      Sunday Times, July 23 1972

2:      'Fair Deal for Housing' HMSO Cmnd 4728

3:      Shields Gazette April 4 1972

4:      Shields Gazette April 29 1972

5:      Ibid

6:      Interview with George Smith

7:      Shields Gazette November 9 1971

8:      Shields Gazette November 20 1971

9:      History of South Shields, Commemorative book, produced by South Shields County Borough Council – 1973

10:     Shields Gazette November 10 1893

11:     'Fighting like Tigers' David Price 1982

12:     Interview with Ivor Richardson

13:     Shields Gazette November 2 1945

14:     Labour Party election leaflet, April 1969, authors private collection

15:     Shields Gazette, May 9 1969

16:     Written correspondence, Stan Smith

17:     Interview with Malcolm Campbell

18:     Shields Gazette, December 31 1971

19:     Written correspondence, George Smith

20:     Shields Gazette, January 13 1972

21:     Conversation with Billy Malcolm

22:     Shields Gazette, January 13 1972

23:     Shields Gazette, March 2 1972

24:     South Shields Labour Party Minute Book, April 4 1972

25:     Shields Gazette, April 5 1972

26:     Shields Gazette, April 6 1972

27:     Shields Gazette, April 27 1972

28:    Interview with Jim Florence

29:    Written correspondence Mike Peel

30:    Interview with Jim Florence

31:    Progressive Party election leaflet, April 1972, authors private collection

32:    Shields Gazette, May 5 1972

Chapter 2 – Local Opposition to the new legislation

1:    Labour Weekly, special issue, published by the Labour Party, December 1971

2:    Shields Gazette, June 28 1972

3:    Ibid

4:    Written correspondence, Jim Riddle

5:    Interview with Liz Diamond

6:    Interview with Jim Doneghan

7:    Interview with Jack Grassby

8:    The Journal newspaper, July 10 1972

9:    Shields Gazette, July 12 1972

10:    Shields Gazette, July 13 1972

11:    Shields Gazette, July 15 1972

12:    The Journal newspaper, July 21 1972

13:    Shields Gazette, July 25 1972

14:    Shields Gazette, July 26 1972

15:    South Shields Trades Council Minutes, 25 July 1972

16:    Shields Gazette, August 10 1972

17:    Shields Gazette, August 11 1972

18:    South Shields County Borough Council Minutes, Management Board, 14 August 1972

19:    Interview with Billy Malcolm

20:    Shields Gazette August 14 1972

21:    Shields Gazette, August 14 1972

22:    Shields Gazette August 18 1972

23:    Interview with Bob Growcott

24:    Shields Gazette, August 16 1972

25:    Shields Gazette, August 18 1972

26:     Shields Gazette, August 23 1972

27:     Interview with Jim Doneghan

28:     Interview with Jack Grassby

29:     Shields Gazette, August 29 1972

30:     Shields Gazette, August 31 1972

31:     South Shields Labour Party Minute Book, August 31 1972

32:     Shields Gazette, September 1 1972

33:     Shields Gazette, August 31 1972

34:     The Journal newspaper, August 31 1972

35:     Felling UDC Town Council minutes, 30 August 1972

36:     Sunderland Borough Council minutes, 31 August 1972

37:     Gateshead Council Housing Committee minutes, 13 September 1972

38:     Shields Gazette, September 2 1972

39:     Conversation with Neil Bonnar

40:     Newcastle City Council minutes, September 6 1972

41:     The Journal newspaper, September 7 1972

42:     Whickham UDC Town Council minutes 7 September 1972

43:     Shields Gazette, September 4 1972

44:     South Shields Labour Party Minute Book, September 5 1972

45:     Interview with Ken Reid

46:     Shields Gazette, September 30 1972

47:     The Journal newspaper, September 28 1972

48:     Shields Gazette, October 2 1972

49:     Interview with Billy Malcolm

50:     Shields Gazette, October 3 1972

51:     Interview with Jim Davison

52:     Interview with Jim Doneghan

53:     Ibid

54:     Interview with Dickie Barry

55:     Shields Gazette October 3 1972

56:     Written correspondence, Stan Smith

57:     South Shields Labour Party Minute Book. October 3 1972

58:     Shields Gazette, October 4 1972

Chapter 3 – The Mandate for resistance

1:     The Story of Clay Cross, David Skinner and Julia Langdon, Spokesman Books, 1974
2:     Shields Gazette October 5 1972
3:     Ibid
4:     Ibid
5:     Ibid
6:     Interview with Billy Malcolm
7:     Interview with Sep Robinson
8:     Shields Gazette October 5 1972
9:     Ibid
10:     Interview with Bob Growcott
11:     Ibid
12:     Interview with Dickie Barry
13:     Shields Gazette October 5 1972
14:     Interview with Dickie Barry
15:     Interview with Bob Growcott
16:     Interview with Malcolm Campbell
17:     Interview with Billy Malcolm
18:     Interview with Bob Growcott
19:     Interview with Dickie Barry
20:     Shields Gazette October 5 1972
21:     Ibid
22:     Ibid
23:     The Journal newspaper, October 6 1972
24:     Shields Gazette October 6 1972

Chapter 4 – The Rent Strike

1:     Shields Gazette October 31 1972
2:     Shields Gazette October 10 1972
3:     Shields Gazette October 23 1972
4:     Shields Gazette October 18 1972
5:     Ibid

6:      Ibid
7:      Interview with Jim Davison
8:      Interview with Malcolm Campbell
9:      Shields Gazette November 7 1972
10:     Interview with Malcolm Campbell
11:     Interview with Bob Growcott
12:     South Shields Labour Party Minute Book, November 7 1972
13:     Shields Gazette, November 6 1972
14:     South Shields Federation of Tenants' Association Leaflet,
        November 1972, authors private collection
15:     Interview with Jack Grassby
16:     Shields Gazette, November 18 1972
17:     Shields Gazette November 20 1972
18:     Ibid
19:     Shields Gazette November 24 1972
20:     Shields Gazette, November 27 1972
21:     South Shields Labour Party Minute Book, December 5 1972
22:     Shields Gazette, December 7 1972
23:     Interview with Malcolm Campbell
24:     Shields Gazette December 7 1972
25:     South Shields County Borough Council Minutes,
        Housing Committee, 6 December, 1974
26:     Shields Gazette December 8 1972
27:     Shields Gazette December 6 1972
28:     Shields Gazette December 11 1972
29:     Interview with Mike Peel
30:     Ibid
31:     Interview with Malcolm Campbell

Chapter 5 – The Revolution delayed

1:      Shields Gazette January 3 1973
2:      Shields Gazette January 11 1973
3:      Shields Gazette January 19 1973
4:      Interview with Jim Riddle

5:      Shields Gazette January 4 1973

6:      Shields Gazette January 9 1973

7:      South Shields Labour Party Minute Book, February 6 1973

8:      Shields Gazette February 3 1973

9:      Shields Gazette February 6 1973

10:     Minutes of the South Shields Trades Union Council,
20 February 1973 and Shields Gazette February 21 1973

11:     Shields Gazette February 19 1973

12:     The Unfinished Revolution, Jack Grassby, TUPS Books, 1999

13:     Written correspondence, Mike Peel

14:     Interview with Bob Growcott

15:     K Sklair, The Struggle against the Housing Finance Act,
Socialist Registar 1975

16:     The Story of Clay Cross, David Skinner and Julia Langdon,
Spokesman Books 1974

17:     B Jacobs, Labour Against the Centre: The Clay Cross
Syndrome – Local Government Studies March/April 1974

18:     Progressive election leaflet, April 1973 – authors private collection

19:     Shields Gazette, March 28 1974

Afterword

1:     South Shields Labour Party Minute Book, February 14 1973

2:     The Unfinished Revolution, Jack Grassby TUPS Books, 1999

3:     Written correspondence, Mike Peel

4:     Labour Weekly, special issue, published by the Labour Party 1971

5:     Shields Gazette, October 11 1972

6:     Dick Taverne, Review Article, The Story of Clay Cross:
Local Government Studies, January 1976

Appendix 2

Letter from Peter Walker, Secretary of State for the Environment, to South Shields County Borough Council

The Town Clerk reported that, arising out of the decision taken by the Board in this matter at their special meeting on the 14th August 1972, a letter dated 1st September 1972 had been received from the Secretary of the Department of the Environment, the full text of which was as follows:-

Your letter of the 16th August about the resolution of your Council's Management Board on the Housing Finance Act has been carefully considered.

It appears that the resolution is based on a misunderstanding of the legal position. The Act places certain statutory duties on Local Authorities. A Local Authority cannot divest themselves of the statutory functions with which they are charged for public purposes. As Local Authorities are in effect the creation of statute, they exist to perform the duties and to exercise the powers conferred upon them by statute. Thus a Local Authority who decides not to perform a duty imposed by the Act are not choosing between two policies which they are free to adopt. They are choosing to act unlawfully instead of lawfully. Neither the fact that remedies exist for a default on a statutory duty, nor the fact that officers of the authority are not being obstructed in carrying out their duties under the Act excuses or mitigates that default in any way.

The Secretary of State may not appoint a Housing Commissioner under the Act unless and until he has made an order declaring an Authority to be in default of certain of their functions under the Act, and the Authority have failed to remedy their default within the time specified in the order. If a Commissioner were appointed, it is likely that there would be conferred on him the housing management functions of the Authority and perhaps other functions as well so that he could effectively remedy the default. He could be involved in introducing and operating a rebate scheme, preparing the provisional assessments of fair rents and applying the provisions for

97

increases towards fair rents. In performing these and any other functions conferred upon him the Commissioner, and not the Authority, would exercise any judgements or discretions and take any decisions required for their performance without reference to the Authority.

If a default order has been made against an Authority, the Secretary of State has power, under Section 99 of the Act, to reduce, suspend, or discontinue any housing subsidy to a Local Authority in respect of any financial year during which he considers the Authority to be in default.

Moreover, if, as a result of negligence or misconduct, the Council were to sustain a loss which could not be made good, the District Auditor would be required by Law to surcharge the Councillors responsible for the negligence or misconduct with the amount of the loss. It is difficult to envisage circumstances in which a vote by a Councillor for a resolution to default on the duties imposed by the Act would not constitute misconduct. It is also in practice almost inevitable that default would lead to some degree of loss. There could be a loss of subsidy. There is very likely to be a loss of income under the Act which the Commissioner ` cannot in practice make good. Moreover the remuneration and expenses of the Commissioner are themselves almost certain to be additional expenditure arising from the default and would constitute a loss.

A Councillor who is surcharged more than £500 is automatically disqualified from election or from being a member of the Local Authority for a period of 5 years, unless the disqualification is removed as a result of an Appeal to the High Court or to the Secretary of State. If more than one-third of the Members of a Council are disqualified at the same time, the quorum necessary to transact the business of the Council is determined by reference to the number of members remaining qualified instead of by reference to the total number of members.

I hope that in view of the explanation of the legal position set out above, your Council will reconsider the resolution which you quoted in your letter.

Appendix 3

The Crucial vote – how they voted

On October 4 1972, South Shields County Borough Council voted by 31-22 in favour of implementing the Housing Finance Act.

The vote was made up as follows:

In favour implementation: 20 Progressives, 11 Labour
Against implementation: 22 Labour
      Abstentions: 3 Labour
      Not Present: 3 Progressive and 1 Labour

FOR

Progressives:

Aldermen: H. Abbey, I. Caplan, E. Hill, Mrs. A. Marsden, G. Maguire, H. Marshall, W. Newby.

Councillors: G. Bairnson (Harton), J. Capstick (Cleadon Park), K. Charlton (Westoe), T. Collins (West Park), J. Crawley (Horsley Hill), S. Curry (Bents), A. Marsden (Beacon), J. McKee (West Park), Mrs. M. Newby (Beacon), Mrs. M. Raffle (Westoe), R. Ramsey (Beacon), S. Smith (Westoe), J. Webb (Harton)

Labour:

Alderman: J. Abbott

Councillors: Mrs. E. Diamond (Brinkburn), M. Diamond (Brinkburn), J. Doneghan (Marsden), R. Donkin (Whiteleas), Mrs. L. Jordison (Simonside), W. Malcolm (Rekendyke), K. Reid (Cleadon Park), D. Ridley (Simonside), K. Webster (Victoria), Mrs. V. Webster (Tyne Dock)

AGAINST

Labour: The Mayor, Councillor V. Fitzpatrick (Marsden)

Aldermen: R. Dodds, G. Gibson, E. Mackley, J. Richardson

Councillors: R. Barry (Rekendyke), T. Bell (Whiteleas), P. Brook (Horsley Hill), P. Cain (Bents), M. Campbell (Rekendyke), J. Davison

(Biddick Hall), J. Dent (Simonside), A. Elliott (Brinkburn), G. Graham (Marsden), B. Growcott (Tyne Dock), J. Hodgson (Cleadon Park), H. Malcolm (Tyne Dock), W. Malcolm (Biddick Hall), Mrs. C. Pearson (Victoria), R. Scott (Horsley Hill), K. Scrimger (Whiteleas), J. Wakeford (Biddick Hall)

ABSTENTIONS

Labour:

Alderman: Mrs. M. Sutton

Councillors: P. Byers (Victoria), Mrs. E. Scrimger (Bents)

NOT PRESENT

Progressive:

Alderman: W. Owen

Councillors: J. Leighton (West Park), M. Lynn (Harton)

Labour:

Alderman: A. Southwick

Appendix 4

Councillor Malcolm Campbell's letter of resignation

77 Lisle Road
South Shields

30ᵗʰ December 1972
The Town Clerk
Town Hall
South Shields

Dear Sir,

You will know that at the last meeting of the Housing Committee I indicated that I felt that I could no longer continue as a Labour Councillor because of the attitude of my Party colleagues to the Tory Rent Act.

It must have been clear for some time that I have been unhappy in my role as Labour Councillor and deeply distressed by the about-face of the Leader of the Labour Group and certain Labour Councillors on their election pledge and public statements.

It has become obvious to me that the power structure of the Party political system on the Town Council allows a small clique to dictate policy contrary to the democratic decision of the majority and in opposition to the expressed views of the electors of the Town. Indeed it has become clear that the political structure has been designed and maintained with this intention.

It has become impossible therefore for me to continue to participate in a system which denies the possibility for me to act in accordance with the socialist principles which I hold and upon which I was elected to the Council.

I should be grateful if you would present this letter of resignation to the Council.

Yours faithfully,

M. Campbell

Appendix 5

Chronology of events

1969

May 8   Progressives take control of South Shields Council and advocate the sale of Council Houses and the selling of Council land.

1970

June 18   Edward Heath becomes Prime Minister.

1971

May 1   Labour gain six seats on South Shields Council — Bob Growcott and Malcolm Campbell are two of Labour's new intake. Progressive majority in the Chamber reduced to two.

Nov 8   South Shields MP Arthur Blenkinsop tells the Commons that old music-hall jokes about Council housing would return as a result of the Governments proposed Housing Finance Act.

Dec 23   Trades Council meets to discuss the effects of the proposed Rent Act.

1972

Jan 12   Housing Committee informed that rent rises of £1 will be needed under terms of Housing Finance Bill. Labour Housing Spokesman Billy Malcolm writes in the Gazette newspaper that the Rent Bill will make housing 'wobble', Progressive Chair of Housing, George Smith says it will make housing 'stable'.

March 1   Labour motion calling for three free-weeks for Council tenants following £200,000 surplus in the rent account is defeated at a full Council meeting by 30 votes to 29.

April 4   Housing Chairman George Smith announces that rents would not be increased until the Finance Bill becomes law and a 'rebate scheme' is in operation. Meanwhile South Shields Labour Party Management Committee agree not to implement Housing Bill, "...if and when the Bill becomes law", Party also agrees to 'honour' Council House sales registered before 4 May if returned to power at the May Council elections.

April 5   Ald. Mackley announces that a Tory Commissioner would need to enter the Town in order to implement the Bill if the Labour Party regains civic control.

April 6	Labour Leader Ernie Mackley urged to resign from the Magistrates Bench by a group of Progressive Councillors following his call that the Labour Party will not implement the Rent Bill.
April 26	A Labour Party motion opposing the Housing Finance Bill is defeated at a meeting of the Town Council. Jim Davison warns that the Bill could lead to the re-emergence of ghettos, Finance Chair John McKee says that 'propaganda' being peddled is making people believe their rents will double.
May 4	Labour gains eight seats in the Council elections and take control of the Authority — Ald. Mackley becomes the Council Leader whilst Billy Malcolm is the new Housing Chairman.
June 27	A meeting organised by the Trades Council Secretary, Jack Grassby, in the Middle Club, agrees to a rent strike if the Bill is implemented in the Town. They also agree to establish tenants groups. Shields Gazette comment says such action is 'illegal'.
June 28	Trades Council sets up a 'Housing Committee' under the Chairmanship of Jim Riddle to organise Tenants Associations and to prepare for a possible rent strike.
July 8	Anthony Crosland advises Labour Councils that the national leadership will not support any rebel Authorities refusing to implement the Rent Bill, if it becomes law.
July 12	Returning from the special Labour Party Conference in London, Ald Mackley urges the Labour Group of Councillors to break its pledge on non-implementation.
July 13	Mackley urged to resign by a Group of Labour Councillors, Party Secretary, Bob Growcott, says he will resign as a Councillor if the Party's non-implementation pledge is broken.
July 14	Mackley survives a vote of confidence at a joint meeting of the Labour Group of Councillors and the South Shields Labour Party Executive Committee — observers claim the vote was 'close'.
July 24	A meeting of the Housing Committee votes against implementation, the Housing Chairman says the decision is 'final'. Committee also rejects taking advantage of the 'Birmingham Clause'.
July 25	Special meeting of the Trades Council Executive Committee welcomes the Housing Committee's decision and agrees to write to Union Branches requesting support if any Labour Councillor faces a financial penalty.

July 26	In a strongly worded 'Comment', the Shields Gazette says that the Council is breaking the law over its refusal to raise the rents.
July 27	Housing Finance Bill receives Royal Assent.
August 10	The Labour Group on the Council votes 13-12 not to obstruct Council Officials preparing for the introduction of the Rent Act — shouts of 'betrayal' and 'collaborators' by non-implementation hard-line Councillors.
August 11	Opposition Leader Stan Smith makes a call for an emergency Council meeting in order to clarify the Council's position on the Rent Act.
August 14	The Council's powerful Management Board, meeting during recess, agrees not to implement the Rent Act but reaffirms the Labour Group's decision not to obstruct officials preparing for the Act — Grassby sends urgent letter to the Labour Party calling for a joint meeting.
August 17	Whiteleas Estate forms a Tenants Association.
August 23	Trades Council warns Labour Councillors to 'keep off tenants groups' and to 'resist the temptation' to take control of them.
August 24	Cleadon Park forms a Tenants Association.
August 25	Shields Gazette reveals dissatisfaction in the Labour Group over its decision not to obstruct officials.
August 30	Labour-controlled Wallsend Council breaks previous pledge and agrees to implement the Act. Labour-controlled Felling UDC votes likewise.
August 31	Special meeting of the South Shields Labour Party votes 37-5 not to implement the Act, meanwhile Labour-controlled Jarrow UDC and Sunderland Borough Councils agree to implement the Act.
Sept 1	In the 'worst night of our lives', Labour-controlled Hebburn UDC votes to implement the Act.
Sept 6	Newcastle City Council votes to implement the Rent Act — the entire Labour opposition votes against implementation.
Sept 7	Whickham UDC votes to implement the Rent Act.
Sept 27	Mackley maintains the Council will not increase rents as Gateshead Council agrees to implement the Rent Act. The South Shields Management Board receives warning letter from Peter Walker, the Housing Minister — the Board reaffirms previous Council Policy.

. South Shields County Borough stands alone amongst the North East Councils.

October 2   Council faces a loss of £16,000 a week over its refusal not to implement the Act. South Shields the only Council in the North East refusing to implement the Act.

A mass meeting in South Shields of 600 people reaffirms opposition to the Rent Act.

Labour Group meets and decides by 17 votes to 15 to allow its members a 'free vote' on implementation, Progressive Leader Stan Smith hails the vote as "the first sign of sanity which has been visible this year."

October 3   South Shields Labour Party Management Committee meets and refuses to discipline any Labour councillor who 'rebels' and votes to implement the Act.

October 4   A stormy meeting of the Council votes 31-22 to implement the Housing Act.

Council Leader Ernie Mackley votes against implementation whilst Housing Chairman Billy Malcolm is among 11 'new' Labour rebels voting for implementation.

October 5   Biddick Hall Labour Councillors Wakeford and Davison resign their Council seats and six Councillors resign the Labour Whip.

October 6   Mackley appeals for unity in Labour's ranks as tenants threaten to oppose Labour nominations at the Biddick Hall by-election.

Party Secretary Bob Growcott retracts decision to resign the Labour Whip and encourages other Councillors to follow suit.

October 17   Meeting of South Shields Trades Council agrees a five-point plan of action drawn up by Jim Riddle, to oppose the Rent Act. Left-wing Hugh Nicol urges a 'retreat with dignity.' by the Trades Council on the issue.

October 31   Progressives announce that George Wilkinson and Eddie Russell will be their candidates in the Biddick Hall by-election.

Nov 3   Labour announces that Jim Davison and Paddy McKay will be their candidates in the Biddick Hall by-election.

Nov 6   Malcolm Campbell criticises the Labour Party selection process at Biddick Hall.

Nov 7   The Rent issue dominates Labour's monthly Management meeting. Party refuses to allow new members to vote during the forthcoming internal selections for 1973 council elections. Jim

Davison and Paddy McKay are affirmed as the official Party candidates to fight the Biddick Hall by-election. The meeting also heavily rejects a motion from the NUM to discipline rebel Councillors. Meanwhile Trades Council distributes leaflets concerning Council's decision and organises a mass meeting.

Nov 18   Mackley tells Council tenants to 'Pay rent rise or be evicted'.

Nov 19   Billy Malcolm assures Trades Council meeting that there will be no mass evictions. Meeting of Tenants Association representatives formally agrees a rent strike.

Nov 20   Rent Strike begins as the rent increase takes effect.

Nov 23   Labour wins the Biddick Hall by-election.

Nov 26   Mass meeting organised to encourage tenants on rent strike.

Dec 5   Monthly meeting of the South Shields Labour Party refuses to allow Malcolm Campbell onto the approved list of possible Labour candidates for the 1973 Council elections — but meeting agrees to allow Cllrs Elliott and Cain onto the list despite still being out of the Labour Group.

          Jarrow Council refuses to meet Low Simonside rent rebels, resistance in the town collapses soon after.

Dec 6   Housing Committee informed that only 295 tenants out of 16,000 are on a rent strike. Malcolm Campbell storms out of a Housing Committee after the meeting refuses to give pledge not to evict rent strike tenants.

Dec 10   Rent strike formally ends with a promise that 'phase two' will commence in February 1973.

1973

January 3   Malcolm Campbell formally resigns from the Council, Stan Smith says that Council tenants were 'badly advised' over the rent strike issue.

January 7   Progressives send a dossier to the District Auditor criticising the Labour Council's handling of the rent issue. Meanwhile Party Agent Jim Doneghan advises unity amongst Labour members.

Feb 20   Trades Council Annual Meeting sees the resignation of Jack Grassby. Communist Jim Riddle replaces him as Secretary; the new President is Malcolm Campbell. In his Annual Report, Grassby accuses local Labour Leaders of a lack of courage and honesty.

April 11   Electors go to the polls to elect their representatives to the new Tyne and Wear County Council. Ernie Mackley heads the poll in Simonside whilst Billy Malcolm tops the poll in Rekendyke.

May 10   Electors go back to the polls to elect their representatives to the new South Tyneside Council. There are no surprises and no independent left-wing candidates. Ernie Mackley again tops the poll in Simonside, whilst Billy Malcolm does the same in Rekendyke.

1974
March 27   The final meeting of South Shields County Borough Council is told that the Council's defiance had resulted in £100,000 not collected in rents with more than £5,620 of this to come out of the General Rate Fund.

Appendix 6

Biographies of Key figures

Alderman Ernie Mackley JP

A mineworker who rose through the Union ranks to become the Treasurer and then Secretary of the Harton and Westoe Miners Lodge Committee. First elected to South Shields County Borough Council (unopposed) in 1945 representing his home ward of Simonside. He was appointed to the Aldermanic Bench in 1958. Mackley succeeded Jack Clark as the Leader of the Labour Group on the Council and then became Council Leader in May 1972 when Labour regained control of the Authority.

Deputy Chairman of the Magistrates Bench, he sought the Parliamentary nomination of South Shields following the retirement of Chuter Ede but lost out to Arthur Blenkinsop.

Elected to the new Tyne and Wear County Council in 1973 (he chose to serve only one term), and also to the new South Tyneside Council in 1973, he became the Chair of the 'Shadow' Authority in May 1973. Defeated in the May 1978 elections by just 36 votes, so bringing to a cruel end over 33 years of public service.
He died in December 1988.

Councillor George Smith CBE

Represented Cleadon Park for the Progressive Association from 1960-1966. He returned to the Council in 1969 for the Tyne Dock ward. Smith became Chair of the Housing Committee when the Progressives seized control of South Shields Council in 1969. He is regarded as one of the architects of the Council's 'Right to buy' policy for Council house tenants and of the sale of Council land for private housing development. An Insurance Claims Assessor by profession, he chose not to seek re-election to the Council in May 1972.

A former Chair of the South Shields Conservative Association, he became a member of the Tyne and Wear County Council in 1973 rising to become Leader of the Conservative group in 1982. His election as a

County Councillor meant that for the first time in the Town's history, the Conservatives had won an election.

George Smith remains today an active member of the local Conservative Association.

Councillor Stan Smith OBE

Like his twin brother George, Stan Smith has a long association with local Council politics. He represented the Westoe Ward as a Progressive from 1959 –73, becoming Leader of the Council when the Progressives gained control of the Authority in 1969.

A former hospital board official, Stan Smith served the Westoe Ward on the new South Tyneside Council from 1973 until 1979. He also served a term for the Conservative Party on Tyne and Wear County Council (1977-81). He was the Conservative Party Parliamentary Candidate in both the February and October 1974 General Elections in South Shields.

He remains an active member of the local Conservative Association in South Shields.

Councillor Billy Malcolm

USDAW trade union activist and local hairdresser whose family have a long association with local politics (his Uncle Billy was first elected in a by-election for the Deans Ward in 1952 and served until 1973, later for the Biddick Hall Ward. His brother Harry was a Tyne Dock Councillor 1966-69 and 70-73 and also served on Tyne and Wear County Council for a term). Like his uncle he was first elected in a by-election for the Rekendyke ward on 29th March 1962. He became Chair of the Housing Committee when Labour regained control of the Authority in May 1972. He was union-supported for the Labour Parliamentary nomination in South Shields following the retirement of Arthur Blenkinsop.

He was elected to the new South Tyneside Council and Tyne and Wear County Council in 1973 (where he served as Vice-Chair of the Finance Committee), but lost his County seat in 1977 and District seat in 1978 (ironically following a massive slum-clearance programme taking place in his ward which resulted in a mass exodus of Labour supporters). He served a final term on the County Council from 1981 until its demise in 1986. He died in 1994.

Two of his sons currently serve on South Tyneside Council.

Jack Grassby

College Lecturer who introduced to South Shields a left-wing campaign style it had never seen before. A brilliant organiser, the local Trades Council under his Secretaryship became one of the most radical in the country.

Despite his being a former Secretary of the South Shields Labour Party, the Party establishment mistrusted him and attempts were made to suspend and even expel Grassby from the local Party. On one occasion he had to fend off a no-confidence motion against him at a meeting of the local Trades Council following claims he had acted without the authority of one of the principal unions.

Politically astute man who levelled his criticism at the Labour Councillors who granted a 'free vote' in the Council Chamber rather than at the eleven who voted to implement the Rent Act.

He resigned the Secretaryship of the Trades Council in February 1973.

Today, Grassby is retired but still plays a role in the local Labour Party.

Councillor Jim Doneghan

Plasterer by trade, elected for the Marsden Ward in 1966. He was regarded as a moderate and pragmatic Labour Party member who (with Ken Scrimger and Liz and Murtagh Diamond) ensured the local Party had its own headquarters in the Town.

Chairman of the Education Committee following Labour's victory at the May 1972 Council elections (Doneghan was the Partys Local Election Agent and organized the election campaign in South Shields), he was an early opponent of the 'non-implementation' strategy but opposed the granting of a 'free-vote' claiming that it was little more than a get-out clause by the Council Leadership.

Elected to the new South Tyneside Council in 1973, he was Deputy Mayor in 1974 but lost his Marsden seat in 1975 after the local newspaper ran a campaign against Councillor's allowances which saw Labour lose a host of seats across the Borough. Doneghan said at the time, "This is the most unusual campaign I have ever fought in".

His wife Evelyn and son Stephen both served terms on South Tyneside Council. He died in 1997.

Councillor Bob Growcott

Local Shipyard worker, Growcott quickly rose to become a highly regarded Secretary of the South Shields Labour Party. He was elected to represent Tyne Dock in 1971 following a hard-fought and controversial campaign against the Progressives. He became Chair of the Council's Environmental Health Committee following Labour's victory in May 1972.

A supporter of the non-implementation strategy who, following the decision to implement the Act, used his position as Party Secretary to keep the Party united in time for the 1973 Council elections.

He was elected to South Tyneside Council in 1973 but chose not to seek re-election in 1978.

He is currently Secretary of a CIU Club in South Shields.

Councillor Dr. John McKee CBE

A prominent local GP, who became Chair of the influential Finance Committee when the Progressives took control of South Shields Council in 1969.

He was first elected to the Council in 1949 (for RARAMA and latterly the Progressives) in Cleadon Park, a seat he held until 1964. He returned to the Council in a by-election on 24th September 1970 for the West Park Ward and remained a Councillor until the demise of South Shields County Borough Council in 1973.

He was the Conservative Party Parliamentary Candidate for South Shields in the 1970 General Election.

He died in June 1999.

Councillor Malcolm Campbell

Taxi-driver and a member of the General and Municipal Workers Union. Campbell was also a Trades Council activist, political ally of Jack Grassby and a staunch supporter of the non-implementation strategy. Commentators today maintain he was the one man ultimately prepared to go to prison over the Act.

First elected in 1971 (ironically for the same ward as the Housing Chair, Billy Malcolm in Rekendyke), he resigned from the Labour Group following the implementation of the Rent Act and eventually resigned from the Authority on 6th December 1972 following the decision of the Housing Committee not to refuse to evict any tenant on a rent strike.

Bore the brunt of the local Labour Partys determination to close ranks after the implementation of the Act. He was expelled from the Labour Group in November 1972 and refused a place on the Party's list of possible candidates for the 1973 elections to the new South Tyneside Authority.

He became disillusioned with Party politics and went to sea, becoming active in the National Union of Seamen. He is now retired but still serves as Chair of the South Tyneside GMB Taxi-drivers Branch.

Councillor Albert Elliott

Mineworker and NUM activist. First elected to represent Simonside in 1966-69 and then Brinkburn 1970-73.

Opponent of the implementation of the Rent Act and was active in the Whiteleas Tenants Association. Resigned the Labour Whip following the decision to implement the Rent Act but was still allowed onto the Labour Party Panel of prospective candidates for the new South Tyneside Council elections following a vote within the Constituency Party.

Regarded as a populist, he stood on the Town Hall steps and announced to the tenants that the rebels had 'sold you down the river' on the night the Council agreed to implement the Rent Act.

Elected to represent Whiteleas in 1973, Elliott is a former Mayor, Chair of Education and also Chair of Housing of South Tyneside Council. He eventually rose to become Leader of the Authority in May 1990.

He died in December 1997 — 'with his boots on'.

Jim Riddle

Tailor and Garment worker, Communist Party activist who rose to become an elected lay Official for Garment Workers Union in Northern Ireland.

Regarded as an extremely able and trusted ally of Jack Grassby. He became the key organiser of the Tenants Associations across South

Shields and chaired the Trades Council Sub-committee responsible for organizing opposition to the Rent Act.

He assumed the Secretaryship of the Trades Council following Grassby's decision to stand down in February 1973.

Now retired, Riddle is active in the Pensioners Movement and a number of voluntary groups on South Tyneside and also within the South Shields Labour Party.

Mike Peel

Mineworker who was active in the NUM and the South Shields Trades Council. Chairman of the Westoe Colliery Mechanics Union, he was also active in the Claimants Union. On the left-wing of the Labour movement, he was Assistant Secretary to Jack Grassby. Peel undertook much of the publicity work needed to highlight the rent strike in the local media.

He left Westoe Colliery to undertake a period of formal study. He is today a highly respected senior Welfare Rights Officer for South Tyneside Council.

Councillors Liz and Murtagh Diamond

A formidable husband and wife team who dominated South Shields Labour politics in the 60s and 70s following the downfall of Ernie Gompertz. Murtagh was a hospital worker and represented the Brinkburn ward from May 1965 until his death in 1980. Liz, a retired headteacher, represented Brinkburn (renamed All Saints) from May 1972 until May 1986.

Right-wing pragmatic stalwarts and pillars of the local Catholic community, they were early opponents of the non-implementation strategy. Murtagh — affectionately known as a 'gentle giant' — was Chairman of the South Shields Labour Party and also Secretary of the Labour Group of Councillors during the Rent Act issue. Liz was a former Secretary of the South Shields Labour and Trades Council and was regarded as the more ruthless. She became Chair of the local Education Authority and is credited with being the driving force behind ensuring the South Shields Labour Party had its own property.

Murtagh died in 1980, Liz died in 1989.

Index

Davison, Jim 16,34,41,43,55,57,60,61,66,77

Dent, John 81

Diamond, Liz 24,41,42,47,50,51,52,62,63,69,72,90

Diamond, Murtaugh 15,24,32,41,42,43,50,57,61,62,72,90

District Auditor 75,76,77,83

Dixon, Don 35

Doneghan, Jim 12,19,24,25,33,41,42,47,48,49,77,90

Downey, Hugh 36

Ede, James Chuter 7,8

Ede House 18

Elliott, Albert 11,24,28,32,51,54,65,68,69,86,

Felling UDC 35,87

Fitzpatrick, Vincent 40,76,77

Florence, Jim 11,17,18,19,69,70

Fry, Jane 11

Gateshead Council 36,39,87

Gibson, George Ald. 53,54

GMWU Trade Union 12

Gompertz, A Ernest 8,9,10

Grassby, Jack 18,21,22,23,24,25,31,32,33,34,42,48,57,64,68,71,73,76, 78,79,80,85

Great Reform Act 6

Growcott, Bob 12,15,26,31,32,51,52,54,55,56,61,80

Heath, Edward 11

Hebburn UDC 13,36

Hepburn, Peter 27

Hodgson, Jim 54,56,69,81

Horsley Hill 8,19,63

Housing Committee 13,14,21,27,68,69,70

Housing Commissioner 16,27,30,39,89

Housing Finance Bill/Act 5,12,13,14,16,19,20,21,23,24,25,26,27,28,29,30, 32,33,34,35,37,40,43,45,47,50,52,57,58,63,69,71,76,81,85,86,87,90

Howard, Brian 71

Ingham, Robert 6

Jarrow UDC 13,35

Jordison, Lillian 12,42

Jounal Newspaper 55

Labour Group of Councilors 21,26,27,28,31,38,39,40,41,42,43,49,53,64, 68,69

Labour Party National Executive 25,60

Labour Party Conference 43

Labour Representation Committee 7

Labour Weekly 87,88

Lansbury George 47,90

Lisle, John 7

Lister, Brian 89

Low Simonside Tenants Association 70

McKay, Paddy 60,61,66

McKee, John 16,46

Mackley, Ernie 8,9,10,15,16,25,26,27,29,30,35,37,38,41,
49,50,52,53,54,64,65,76,77,82,85,86,87,88,90

Malcolm, Billy 8,14,15,19,21,28,30,32,40,45,47,48,50,51,53,54,65,66,69,
76,81,82,83,86

Malcolm Harry 11,82

Mali, Alderman 35

Management Board 30,38,45,49,76,83

Marshall, Harry 84

Maxwell, A D 31

Moderate 8,10

Municipal Representation Committee 7

National Union of Public Employees (NUPE)

NALGO 78

National Union of Mineworkers 13,17,63,73

Newcastle Council 26,37,87

Nicol, Hugh 17,59,71,78

North Eastern Housing Association 37,39

NUTGW Union 17,24

Peel, Michael 17,18,19,22,71,72,80,85

Poll Tax 86

Poplar Guardians 47,90